UNCOMMON
SENSE

- The State is Out of Date -

Gregory Sams

LONDON

Published in Great Britain by

CHAOS WORKS
2 Trevelyan Gardens
London NW10 3JY
website: www.xaos.demon.co.uk

ISBN 0 9531301 0

First edition- Aug 1997
Second printing- Dec 1997
Third printing - May 1998 revised and expanded launch edition

A CIP catalogue record for this book is available from the British Library.
The Author asserts the moral right to be identified as the author of this work.

Printed and bound by Biddles Ltd
Guildford, England

Contents

Perhaps the sentiments contained in the following pages are not yet sufficiently fashionable to procure them general favor; a long habit of not thinking a thing **wrong**, gives it a superficial appearance of being **right**, and raises at first a formidable outcry in defence of custom. But the tumult soon subsides. Time makes more converts than reason.

From Thomas Paine's
Introduction to "Common Sense" - 1776

Preface

I have chosen Paine's quote to lead this preface, since he has put the sentiments so well that I wish to express to the reader. The notion that tradition of itself gives validity should continually be questioned. The Egyptians kept slaves for thousands of years; for centuries it was tradition to bind women's feet in China; for nearly two thousand years it was believed that the whole universe rotated around the earth at its centre. Perhaps our reaction to traditional practice is like the naive belief of young children that all adults must know what they're talking about, since they've been around for so long.

As a child I remember thinking it perfectly plausible that if it was possible for one person to bring about a great World War, as it seemed Hitler had recently done, then it must be possible for one man to bring about a great World Peace. I know better now.

Jesus, Mohammed and other prophets and interpreters of divine truth sought to give us some pointers to peace but the religions that developed after they died have not yet brought peace and brotherhood to mankind. Most religions are still based on the premise that, if only we would all follow the exact same version of the divine interpretations of one particular prophet, then we would have world peace and global harmony. But people are different and times change.

Like many, I used to hope that one day some inspired leader might come along, political or spiritual, and that somehow this person would get the ball rolling in the right direction and unite us all behind them and their pure inspired actions. Perhaps some combination of Christ, Gandhi, the Buddha and Richard Branson would do the trick. In despair of this miracle ever arising on earth, some even hope for an imminent Alien Contact with a Ten Commandments type of scenario broadcast simultaneously in all languages to all televisions and radios around the globe. But would even this, an ultimatum from space, do the job?

After many years' consideration it now seems clear to me that whilst one person's actions can demonstrably plunge chunks of the world into war and disorder, a state of peace can never be constructed or created by the action of a single person. It may come as a surprise to discover that a state of peace is as much the natural condition of our world as is the stability that develops in the natural rainforest. A state of balance and harmony arises as the eventual result of billions of people's activities and interests interacting with each other, and the rest of the world, in a free condition. One person or group of people, however chosen and however enlightened or inspired, cannot determine the specific route to this state of peace. And somewhere in our soul we know that peace is a possible condition - something that our species is capable of achieving, notwithstanding our lengthy catalogue of failures.

I suggest that is not a natural condition of being human that we must kill and maim each other for really unnecessary reasons. After meeting thousands of people in travels across different continents, cultures, and sub-cultures, I have formed the opinion that the vast majority of humanity are not natural-born killers.

Our incessant attempts to forcibly put order into the chaotic and constantly changing mix of our civilization is the reason, I suggest, that we experience so much disorder, suffering and what is often referred to as "chaos". For too long society has been "run" on the basis that we are actually able to govern and control something so complex by setting ever more complex rules and regulations - linear controls which often serve to obstruct the natural evolutionary changes that a successful development of our species demands.

This book is not all about some dramatic new way to run the world. It is unlikely that there is a way this can be achieved according to a plan, dictated from "above". The world can look after itself and support us if we work within its basic operating framework, which is a fundamentally free system. The reason we threaten the future of the planet that sustains us is because we have become a significantly dominant species and yet still work in ignorance of one of the most basic operating principles of the universe - one that has recently been recognized in the new science known as "chaos theory" (Ch.4).

There is a way not to run the planet and it might seem self-evident that the way it is being done today is a good example. Nevertheless, the usual approach to this situation is to assume that a change of figurehead or even a severe re-arrangement of the knobs and levers, will sort things out eventually. These pages will seek to convince you that no new combination or rearrangement of the complex controls of coercive power will work. Consider the number of states there are in the world, each run by people who believe they know what they are doing and each tweaked to its local circumstances. Now consider the minor and major tweaking that has gone on throughout the history of the state (pharaoh, church, senate, king, emperor, president, military junta, parliament, etc.). It is apparent that there have already been many many thousands of different combinations attempted. None of them have worked in the long term, though some lasted more years than others.* Now do we really believe that, for instance, Version 273,583 is going to be the one that finally works?

*Though the empires of the pharaohs or the Romans were long-lived by today's standards, they existed on conquest or subjugation, and when they finally changed they did so in a collapse from grandeur to obscurity, losing most of the culture and civilization that had been developed.

At the time each new government or state takes control, it was generally believed by the instigators/originators of this new state that they had the right policies and programmes to get everything working just perfectly or at least a lot better. Should these programmes collapse or fail, as they have usually done throughout history, the blame is most often placed on "outside influences" - starkly showing the inability of these statesmen to recognise that we all inhabit the same small planet. I will seek to convince you that there are far too many complex elements involved in the system we call society and civilization, for any group of people to determine its course and evolution with coercively-backed regulations and rules, made either locally or globally, made with good intent or bad.

The state does perform functions that are necessary to society. It claims the monopoly on these vital functions and does an increasingly bad job of them. We can see crime proliferating as more and more money is spent combating it. We see our true health decline as more and more is spent on sickness care by the state. The notion that more hospital beds and doctors are the sign of a successful "health policy" is the sign of a sick nation. In education, agriculture, the roads, social security, nuclear power - wherever we look, the determined hand of the state can be seen to twist and distort that which it seeks to improve.

My proposition is that the means to deal with vital functions can and eventually will arise in a freely operating society so that, for example, thieves and murderers do not run amok, nor polluters have a free license to destroy our environment. Whilst we need mechanisms to deal with these areas, it is apparent that the current mechanism upon which we rely is proving inadequate. The state, local and national, is far more diligent and effective at raising taxes than it is at pursuing polluters, crime, graft or corruption. Many of the state's laws are unnecessary in any event, filling our courts and prisons with perpetrators of crimes that have no real victims. A free society would have no difficulty with many things now thought to be unacceptable by the state. It could tolerate herbalists, street traders, gambling clubs (we live with the Lottery), prostitution and many forms of activity and enterprise now banned, discouraged or licensed. Much of what consenting adults do with their own bodies and minds, in their own time, is still regulated by criminal law. There are many nations where homosexuals are jailed, or those who question the prevailing religion or state.

The state's priorities will not change. As you will see, self-interest, self-survival and self-advancement will always be the primary concern of any ruler or government and of the individual power exercisers who are manipulating the controls. The next election will always be the politician's foremost consideration. The short-term interests of society will take a poor second best, with our long-term interests hardly considered. When a government is said to be "in power" it holds that power for the simple reason that it has the ability to force us to do or not do that which it decides is best. I will argue that whether this power was won in a political bunfight or brutally acquired through military force, it makes little difference in the long run. Once a new state is seen to have a firm grip upon the reins of power, the world will recognize it and welcome it to the family of nations.

There are more questions than answers in this book and more problems aired than solutions given. This is not a pessimistic view, but one based on the premise that our current methods of attacking the problems of the world actually block the emergence of organic working solutions. Nor will every aspect of every subject be aired, or copious examples delivered on every principle. The intention is to stir the pot rather than draft a finished recipe with measured ingredients. Were I to cite evidence supporting each point or assertion, then many of these chapters would fill an entire book, and sentences stretch to entire chapters. You can view it as a jigsaw puzzle with a few of the pieces missing. The picture is there, and as you see it you will be in a better position to fill in the missing pieces yourself. Do not be a slave to anyone else's thought just because they make a good argument. Think for yourself - it's your life.

> *"We are usually convinced more easily by reasons we have found ourselves than by those which have occurred to others."*
>
> *Pascal (1623-1662)*

*This book is dedicated
to the future evolution
of our wonderful
species.*

1. What Would an Alien Think?

Just for a moment, imagine humanity from the viewpoint of some alien consciousness at least as developed as ours, but without the imposed order of state control as a focusing element of its evolution and culture. This intelligence may have music, dance, art, design, cuisine, architecture, communication, science, love, fashion, high technology, clubs, pubs, sports, humour, drama, means of travel, animal friends and all the other changing elements we treasure in our own culture. After all, none of them were conceived, planned or developed by the state, though from time to time the state may seek to influence, support or control different aspects of them for the supposed benefit of us all.

OK, you assume that this alien must have a central commander and head of state even though they are not needed for any of the above cultural achievements, nor even to build spaceships. You assume this because central command is all that we have in our own limited frame of reference. It certainly IS NOT the natural state. You have only to look around you to realise that every other intelligent life form which shares this Earth with us has operated successfully for millennia without any form of central controlling structure for the species. The dinosaur dominated for thirty five times the period that we have been on the planet, as far as we know without the benefit of any parliament, king or other ruling body.

As far as I am aware, even ants have no central code of law defining specific punishments for ants that step out of line. In their specific "one-mind" type of community however, it is likely that any ant choosing not to contribute in the expected manner would soon lose the support of its colony and therefore die. I know of no voting council of trees which determines the specific proportions and varieties of trees in a given forest. It is notable that in many cases, such as the oak,* the long-term successful species has figured out how to co-operate with as many other species as possible. This ability to co-operate with other forms of life is a far more intelligent long-term survival strategy than is that of domination and control by rulers and ruling bodies. We sometimes forget that there are many more wildebeest and impala than there are lions and tigers.

*The oak tree acts as a mini-biosphere for up to 300 other varieties of life-form.

Why do we assume that some other intelligent species, even more "successful" than us, will have the same sort of flawed structures as ourselves, with different names for the leaders and lawmaking bodies? Why is it so inconceivable to us that any other civilization could be operating, as does every successful structure in the universe - in a state of freedom? These aren't deep questions - they just reveal the deep ruts in which our own imagination is trapped.

We also assume that any intelligent creature capable of space travel will come equipped with ray guns, ionic blasters, phaser bolts and a full arsenal of high-tech. weaponry with which to kill and destroy. Why? We humans have experienced a dramatic and possibly unique evolution of ways to kill each other on this planet. A mainstay of our chosen cultural entertainment involves depictions of us killing each other in countless war and confrontational movies. Are we to assume that this is a normal or natural element of any highly developed civilisation?

Our alien may have learned how to travel along the fractal patterns of hyperspace and be able to outmanoeuvre a missile or fighter jet. But it is quite possible that its civilization never figured out how to split the atom. Maybe it never had the fear of a Hitler to inspire its scientists to tap such a destructive force. The consequences of this discovery appear to have been universally negative and now pose an added threat to our own survival. Yet we assume that a higher alien intelligence will have even greater means of destruction at its disposal. This is a basically illogical assumption. More destructive power is neither the hallmark of higher intelligence nor the key to peace and stability.

We assume that our highly developed alien will have a very highly developed state and well regulated society. Yet what does the central controlling state actually give to us, not one specific state here or there, but the beast in general - the totality of states running their own big and little countries around the world? They primarily exist to protect us from other versions of themselves. It is difficult to find anything else they do which we treasure, or are satisfied by. They take vast sums of money from us and piss back a little here and there, sprinkling some on the poor and hungry if they are left wing, or subsidizing the unworthy and unnecessary if they are right wing. The vast majority of it though, whichever wing of the bird the centre tilts toward, is wasted and squandered in useless, unproductive and often downright damaging activities.

Probably 80% of what the state does is unnecessary or unproductive, things we are quite capable of sorting out in society without resort to one ruling body, supported by police, the military, nuclear arsenals, parliaments, dictators, presidents and vast armies of bureaucrats. I refer to things such as which side of the road we drive on, what size packet our pasta is sold in, how we generate electricity, what constitutes an acceptable dwelling or house, how two people make a commitment to each other, what types of medicine we use, or how long can we work in a week. Don't imagine that we would live in some disordered mess without a central command issuing all these rules. Wherever they don't exist in our society we seem to have developed real order. We will read more about the reliable aspects of our culture that developed from its own chaotic interactions rather than by government directive.

The other 20% of the state's frame of activities consists of valuable and necessary functions. Unfortunately, the state does a lousy job in these areas and it is getting worse rather than better. These functions include arenas that vary from state to state, but usually include some mix of essential areas such as education, roads, health care, power, protection from crime, safety regulation, charity, transportation or the press. The state does not govern these areas, it seeks to control them to the best of its abilities.

So what happened to our alien? Well, I hope that he or she will spend enough time to feel a sense of awe for the beauty of this planet and for many of the wonderful technological and cultural achievements arising from our own unique evolution through the chaos of society. But, if our alien is intelligent, it would not take it very long to recognise that Planet Earth is a dangerous place for its own massively armed human inhabitants, let alone a relatively peaceful creature visiting from another world.

We can understand why our visitor might have reticence about "coming out" in our civilization, and frequently may need to "hyperspace" it back to a civilization whose inhabitants had long ago found peace and stability without the need to continually control and kill each other in its pursuit. They will also, perhaps, have found ways to do this without raping and damaging the ecosystem that supports them.

And I think it unlikely that our alien would willingly choose to share the secrets of space travel with us.

Disclaimer: Readers are advised not to accept lifts in any unidentified spaceships. The author has no idea who or what is "out there" and simply uses "our alien" as a vehicle for taking a different perspective of our own system - and to discourage the assumption that the way we earthlings run society is a natural thing.

*"We shall get nowhere until
we start by recognising that
political behaviour is largely
non-rational, that the world
is suffering from some kind
of mental disease which must
be diagnosed before it can be
cured."*

George Orwell (1903 - 1950)

2. The Emperor has no Clothes

We all know the story of the little boy who realised not only that the emperor was wearing no clothes, but also acknowledged that he saw it, and said so, even though everybody else was acting exactly as if the emperor did have his clothes on. Today it is apparent that big government, the state, has lost any of the merit that we imagine it had in "the old days." Deep inside, more and more of us realise that our structure of government by the state is a decaying system and all over the world we read daily of its latest dire activities against our civilization and of past abuses now revealed.

The term "for political reasons" is commonly taken to mean that something is not being done for genuine reasons. Politicians rate below even lawyers in numerous surveys that gauge public respect for different professional groups.* Our own cultural "body language" tells us what we really think of politics. Most of us have far greater confidence in our corner grocer or our carpenter than we do in our government - those who profess to be supplying us with the essential need of running our society and protecting our borders. It is sobering to recognize that few of those who claim the ability to run our country would be able to successfully manage a corner grocery store in the marketplace they have distorted. Few of us can look in our souls and really believe that the state, our government system, is working.

> *"Government is not reason. Government is not eloquence. It is force. And, like fire, it is a dangerous servant and a fearful master."*
>
> *George Washington first US President (1732 -*

* A Jan. 1997 survey indicated that 95% of Pakistanis believe most politicians to be corrupt. Of course, each of the parties in the election about to take place was promising to clean up corruption. According to the respected English language "Herald" newspaper the respondents were unanimous in seeing bureaucrats as the most corrupt group.

Yet most of us go about our daily lives acting as though the emperor does indeed have on his new clothes - heatedly comparing one politician's outfit to another's, wishing they would "do something effective" about this or that problem, bemoaning the billions wasted on shelved missile projects and failed employment schemes and thinking that it is somehow going to stop happening.

We refuse to recognise openly that the emperor has no clothes because the alternatives seem so horrific. If the emperor is really naked then:

- who will run the emergency wards?
- who will pay the unemployed?
- who will maintain employment in the arms industry?
- who will keep our streets safe?
- who will make sure our air is not poisonous?
- who will safeguard the farming industry?
- who will educate our children?
- who will insure the nuclear power industry?
- who will decide what foods and drugs are safe?
- who will look after us when we can't look after ourselves?

These may be important and vital issues but the size of the issue and the need for action should not blind us to the obvious. The archaic/modern state does not deliver what it promises when it moves in to control these vital issues. This seems to be the case whether we are talking about Uncle Sam, the Taliban, the former Soviet Union or present day Russia. I would be interested to hear of any country in the world where, in private, a majority of the inhabitants are genuinely satisfied with their government's efforts.

Of course, so many of the terrible problems which we depend upon

> "Politicians are, in fact, in the business of getting and keeping power and everything else is subordinate to that.
>
> As I have grumbled before, there is no such thing as 'good government,' certainly not in the sense that some businessmen look for it. There is a lot of government and there is a little government. If you are lucky, you get the latter. We are unlucky."
>
> Andrew Alexander - Jan. 1997

governments around the world to deal with, are problems that are caused by governments around the world. It is the state in general, our protecting Emperor, which carries out, sanctions or aggravates the activities that create orphans, refugees, terrorists, the homeless, famines, bankrupts, bulging jails, unsupported families, many of the unemployed and even mad cows, as we shall see...

"The budget should be balanced. Public debt should be reduced. The arrogance of officialdom should be tempered, and assistance to foreign lands should be curtailed, lest Rome become bankrupt."

Marcus Tullius Cicero, 63 B.C.

3.   The State is Out of Date

Some writers have so confounded society with government, as to leave little or no distinction between them; whereas they are not only different, but have different origins. Society is produced by our wants, and government by our wickedness; the former promotes our happiness positively by uniting our affections, the latter negatively by restraining our vices. The one encourages intercourse, the other creates distinctions. The first is a patron, the last a punisher.

Thomas Paine, COMMON SENSE - 1776

Little has changed in the management of the state for four thousand years.* Whether we are told what to do by pharaohs, emperors, priests, generals, senates, kings, presidents or democratically elected representatives, the resultant state operates on the same basic principles of legislating change with coercively supported laws. These should not to be confused with natural laws such as those of gravity and thermodynamics. Instead of relying upon willing "customers" or popular support for its public service, the state has always funded itself with coercively raised taxes or plunder from other nations. As we will see in the next chapter, these principles of state management are now shown to be flawed and destined to ultimately fail whenever and for whatever purposes they are applied.

*It was about 2000 BC that the history begins of city states, armed marauders and organized systems of government and belief.

Maybe there was a time when the state was the lesser of two evils - when it was necessary to have strong men willing to kill on command in order to protect us from the bakers, tailors and farmers living over the hill or across the river. Today however, in most of the world's frightening conflicts, the danger comes from the confrontation between those who have control of a territory, and those who seek to wrest it from them. Maybe civilization did get a boost from some of the stability that early governing states were able to achieve. We certainly know that rulers today and in the past have always taken credit for the achievements of civilization that occurred during their reign.* Yet, too often we have seen a large part of that civilization's achievements destroyed with the state when it is eventually conquered,** or decayed and dissipated by the time that it falls of its own weight. This happened dramatically in the former Soviet Union which ultimately fell apart from the weight of its own uselessness, without any actual penetration or provocation from outside forces or agencies. The world is full of the magnificent ruins of civilizations past - the temples, statues and fortresses that remain as the monuments to the pomp and paranoia of rulers past. Had the Romans invented dynamite it is unlikely that even these would remain.

*England's erstwhile former Prime Minister John Major sought to take credit in 1996 for London's image as a swinging city, despite his governments steadfast efforts to control and ban most of the behaviour that makes London swing. His successor displays the same hypocrisy with the "Cool Britannia" theme.

**Much of the knowledge of earlier civilizations was lost when the great library of Alexandria was burnt as a battlefield tactic. Great cities such as Carthage and Constantinople were razed to the ground. Most of Archimedes' knowledge was lost in the taking of Syracuse.

The main reason most of us believe it necessary to have a state "of some sort" centrally controlling society is because we think it to have always been done that way and therefore it has to be done that way. Who else would decide which side of the road we drive upon, or what to do with murderers, or what are safe chemicals to add to the food chain? The fact that our road programme has gone berserk, that murder and incidental violence continue to grow, and that our food chain is dangerously polluted rarely comes to mind when we consider with horror the void that we imagine would be left without "central control" telling us all just what we need to do and making damn sure we do it - or else!

In practice, we can see from history that this management of the system by dictate has not worked so far, and now we can both see why and understand that it could never be possible. Yet we are so used to its inefficiencies, iniquities and regular horrors that we accept it with resignation as the way of the world - a necessary evil. It does not seem to matter much whether the state is run by good men or bad - or run by women. It does not seem to matter whether it gets power by divine right, inheritance, struggles for freedom or democratic elections. When every state comes to its inevitable demise, those elements of society that it has been controlling most are generally those in the greatest disarray.

And yet we still somehow believe that without this system in place there would be a terrible void, gross disorder and a degeneration of society into some kind of a violent morass ruled by the whim of the mob.

In fact, as we will see, most aspects of society that we can currently depend upon, evolved outside of this state-run system - things such as our food supply, communications and entertainment which were neither planned nor centrally controlled, but work just fine.

Yet the state's modus operandus is to determine just what is a *standard* standard-of-living and then try to legislate us all into it, either by supporting people who have not reached the ideal standard, or by attacking those who choose some other way to live. Why should we let officials of the government be responsible for our living standards, when so many of the problems they deal with are caused by them, or would not be seen as a problem to anyone else but them?

In a sense the state, like slavery or war, has always been a very flawed concept. It doesn't work, has never worked and is not in the long-term interest of our society, our civilization or our own personal evolution.

"It has been said that democracy is the worst form of government except all those other forms that have been tried from time to time"

Winston Churchill, 1947

That said, it seemed like a reasonable way to run things - especially when everybody else was doing it. But we haven't found a way to make it work in four thousand years and we threaten our very existence with our persistence in putting new clothes on the Emperor. Four thousand years is not a long time in our own evolution on this planet, which may have spanned anything up to two million years or more.

We are now faced with some clear evidence that this system cannot work. The one constant feature binding the states that have been trying to run the world for four thousand years is the foundation stone of DETERMINISM. Determinism is, quite simply, the belief that by central planning, with the right information, you can determine the actual development of a complex system. It is the belief that by passing man-made laws and launching programmes and plans we can more positively affect and effectively control the evolution of society than it can do by itself. This, we now know, is like saying we could do a better job of managing the solar system by adjusting and carefully regulating the orbits and rotations of each of its planets, moons and asteroids. What science can do with some regularity is determine, in the sense of correctly predicting, what a complex system is going to do, or guess the probability of various possible outcomes. What it cannot do is alter or

accurately influence the outcome of the system by mandate, combined
with manipulation of some of its parts.

The new discoveries of science provided by the study of chaotic systems shows us not only that efforts to mechanistically control them are
futile, but also that they have an organizing force of their own. That is
to say that chaotic systems, **systems with an uncountable number of
parts operating independently in an unpredictable manner,*** have
a fundamental tendency to organize themselves into stable and flexible
working systems, constantly adjusting themselves according to feedback from within and without the system. The information that fuels
this process is the continual exchange between all of the system's infinite components, feeding back information and reaction from one to
another. This is portrayed as a system made up of multiple-layered
"feedback loops" weaving patterns at all levels throughout - organizing
themselves around things called "strange attractors."

*This is the definition that I use for a chaotic system - there may well be other
ways to describe it.

A good example of such a system is the rain forest, which creates a
stable system sustaining the existence of its myriad components, while
delivering oxygen to the rest of the globe as a by-product. Another
manifestation of chaos organizing itself is the evolution of music in our
society, evolving through constantly new harmonies, forms and tech-
nologies in order to provide continually new variations of pleasure for
billions of differently tuned ears. Without any central plan, the system
manages to keep up with what the complex system (culture's musical
tastes).

We could worry much less about the fate of the Amazonian rainforest, were the Brazilian state not actively subsidising clearance for cattle
ranching, as well as building roads and facilities for Japanese timber
interests. One of the "jokes" in the rain forest is: "Where's the beef," as
many contractors simply clear the land, take the subsidy money and
run, rather than sticking around for the precarious business of trying to
feed cattle on the thin topsoil that is exposed. The state, in its brazen
desire to expand its effective tax base, spends great sums of so-called
public money to entice business to rape an ecosystem that would economically otherwise remain untouched. Though the whole project
bears all the hallmarks of a disaster that will be forever regretted, it
could be doggedly pursued for years by a state which will always have
successors to be responsible for its short-sightedness.

And just imagine if our society believed music to be so important to our lives that it had to be regulated, like housing, with strict government controls and regulation. Would we ever have had jazz, rhythm & blues, rock 'n roll, the Beatles, punk rock, acid house, ambient music, or techno in any of its growing manifestations? The state of the music industry in France today is a testament to that government's absurd attempts to legislate the content of music and maintain its French "cultural integrity." They have at least excluded classical music from their complex regulations since many of the great composers were not French.

That the state is unable to deterministically manage a system as complex as human society is evident in every area over which they exert control. A classic case in Europe is the Common Agricultural Policy which - through trying to safeguard our food supply - has come to

EU urged to drop farming subsidies

A high-powered panel of experts yesterday advocated a massive withdrawal of state support from Europe's heavily subsidised farmers and said they should become much more competitive.

The new Minister of Agriculture, Douglas Hogg,

Guardian - Jul 1995

Variations on this story have appeared several times per year for the past decade or two. But who dares "bell the cat"?

author's note

pose the greatest threat to it and our health. Some of the effects of the Common Agricultural Policy are:

• It counters our evolutionary change to a healthier diet, by interfering with the essential and effective feedback loop supplying information from the consumer to the producer. Subsidizing farmers and producing according to central decision-making badly interferes with the natural information exchange. The Soviets tried to do it.

• It encourages the introduction of toxic chemicals to our ecosystem through supporting and subsidising food production beyond society's demands. Much of the use of toxic chemicals and treatments is, when not mandated, certainly encouraged by the state's guarantee to purchase, or subsidize the sale. This lowers the quality of our food.

• It is responsible for the surplus of cattle that were fed back to themselves, as a means of reducing the "beef mountain." This created the conditions for the growth and spread of BSE (mad cow disease). The original cause of this modern tragedy is the intervention of the state in our food chain. The main alternative theory points to the effects of a state-mandated painting of all British cattle with a highly toxic lotion covering the head and spinal column.

• It has been cited by regular studies as unworkable, corruption-prone and grossly inefficient since the early 1980's. Literally billions of pounds, our pounds, are scammed and lost every year as this out-of-control creation of Brussels gets on with its regular job - which itself has little merit.

Yet somewhere in Brussels, nerve-centre of the growing European Empire, the wielders of deterministic power think that some more of our money and some clever manipulation of the grotesque formula will get it all working. The alternative of lost jobs (their own) and responsi-bilities is too awful to contemplate. We will have more on the above points later. I leave it to researchers and historians to determine, but suggest that almost any large empire, in the final 10% of its existence, has more priests and bureaucrats and military, with more volumes of laws and regula-tion, than at any other point in the 90% of the rest of its existence. I suggest that this applies as much to the Aztec Empire as to the Roman Empire, the former Soviet Union or to the world's cur-rent last-surviving superpower.

> *"Corruptissima republica plurimae leges."*
>
> *The worse the state, the more laws it has."*
>
> *Tacitus 55 - 120 A.D.*

People may plan their lives ahead and often live out the plan suc-cessfully, companies can plan five-year strategies and projects that may come to fruition. But in neither instance is civilisation as a whole forced to accept these plans, and they stand or fall on their own merit. Should someone in Japan develop a car that runs on water, then all the plans of the oil companies will need rapid alteration. They are part of the chaotic mix of billions of entities making decisions that affect all of the other entities on the planet in unpredictable ways - the ways of a complex system. If they do fit in and positively enhance our lives they survive and prosper.

Our newly discovered scientific appreciation of the nature of chaotic and complex systems (see next chapter), gives us a clear explanation for the eventual failure of all past and future government programmes involving the forced manipulation and management of "vital" aspects of the complex system that is our society. In every area that the state controls, the natural feedback loop inherent in a complex system is broken. We cannot expect "our say" at the ballot box to make more than a marginal difference to things. We know that whoever is in power will be ineffectual and a waste of our money - and yet we continue to avoid even wondering if there are possible alternatives to the palpable madness of the modern state, democratic or otherwise.

In this book, we accept that, however the controls are rearranged, the state is never going to be able to legislate the world into peace, harmony and progress. It appears to have no positive part to play in the healthy or successful evolution of our species and its own activities are indeed counter-evolutionary. It does not work and many now realize this, accepting it only as a necessary evil. But there it is - what to do? First of all - *stop* believing that the state is necessary, *stop* being frustrated by its inevitable failures and *stop* expecting that it will get something right in the long run. By realizing that the state is not a viable option, we open ourselves up to the discovery of alternative forms of managing our society.

> *"I think that people want peace so much that one of these days government had better get out of the way and let them have it.*
>
> *...Every warship, every tank and every military aircraft built is, in the final sense, a theft from those who are hungry and are not fed, from those who are naked and not clothed."*
>
> Dwight D. Eisenhower, Allied Military Commander World War II and US President 1952-1960

> *"What luck it is for governments that the people they rule do not think."*
>
> HITLER, circa 1940

"Three times in his speech President Bush recited that now familiar phrase 'new world order.' ...the trouble is that order is a 19th century concept. It suggests Metternichian arrangements of large, heavy, somewhat static entities. **History in the late 20th century seems to belong more to chaos theory and particle physics and fractals;** it moves by bizarre accelerations and illogics, by deconstructions and bursts of light."

TIME MAGAZINE - March, 1991

4. Chaos Theory

Most people are understandably frightened by the daily headline connotations of the word chaos, used synonymously with disorder and disruption. This is not what the science dubbed "chaos theory" is about, and there is not any one theory to it - any more than there is one theory to physics or biology. Chaos theory explains how a rainforest achieves stability and balance without anybody centrally programming what grows where and why. It shows us that the wild chaos of the rainforest, with no imposed control, manages to succeed as a "happy" rainforest - unless bulldozed by the state. Chaos theory defines a new attitude to the world that science studies; it has created and stimulated many new branches of science called complexity theory, anti-chaos theory, co-chaos, dynamical systems theory, non-linear dynamics and other less provocative titles. Chaos theory has enabled the existing sciences - whether biology, geology or physics - to look at the wholeness of their subject rather than just smaller and smaller subsections of it. Chaos theory also explains why the synchronicity that so often astounds us in life is, indeed, just another manifestation of the patterned web that connects our universe together.

This book refers to chaos theory and specifically to the implications it has for our approach to the management of our own affairs. However, most of it will ring true to your own experience of life, whether or not science had ever discovered the patterned dynamics that self-organize within a complex system. Though a small library has been written on the multiplying dimensions of this new science, there appear to be few scientists who have looked through its lenses at the way in which we deterministically run our society. Scientists do have to beware of lost government funding and career's possibly damaged by straying into areas that have traditionally not been the province of science. The most ardent proponents of chaos theory will rightly explain the linkage between today's hurricane and a butterfly's wingflap in Guatemala six months ago. Yet few of them would look seriously at a possible linkage between the connections proposed by astrology, or accept that indications of our nature and tendencies are shown in the lines of the hand. The implications of chaos theory for the way in which we govern our society ultimately hold the greatest benefits for us and, ironically, are the ones that could take the longest for the scientist to explore.

The origins of this science, spawned in the 1970's, are briefly explored here, but it is not the purpose of this book to dazzle you with all the implications of its growing usage in image compression, financial forecasting, mineral prospecting, medicine, image creation, traffic flow dynamics, data encryption and so on. Suffice it to say here that chaos theory has given scientists the tools and understanding needed to see what is happening in a far bigger picture than they could ever see before. There are many benefits of this already becoming manifest.

The focus of this short book is on us, all of us together, for we are all part of a complex system in which **anything affects everything**. We will look at the usual world in a different way, forgetting for a moment much of what we have always taken for granted. The human race has not been on this planet nearly long enough for anyone to seriously argue that something must be a done a certain way, "because that's the way it's always been done." We have existed for less than 5% of the time-span that the dinosaurs lived on earth, and have just discovered a science that clearly shows why our short and probably recent experimentation with different coercive structures and techniques through which to rule society, has not yielded a long-term* successful formula yet.

*By "long-term" I simply mean something which goes on working and adapts to changing circumstances and, if replaced, is done so by an improved version.

There is no $E = mc^2$ type of equation to sum up the essence of chaos theory, though the formula most likely to be identified with it is the elegantly simple one which reveals the infinite world of the Mandelbrot set: $Z = z^2 + c$. The discovery of chaos theory has given science the tools and the inclination to study the overall patterns and the form of the phenomena being studied, with less emphasis on reducing the subject into smaller and smaller pieces in which are found even smaller bits. Believe it or not, science has discovered the concept of the whole!

In pre-Babylonian times Chaos was perceived as the mysterious space between Heaven and Earth, and the source of inspiration, form and change in this world. Surprisingly, this is closer to today's scientific usage of the word than that in the newspapers. The quantum shift to a deterministic attitude, and the belief that man had dominance over the earth, appears to have taken place around 2000 BC for most of the emerging civilizations we know about today - our approximate period of history. This shift is classically depicted in the Babylonian myth in which Marduk, symbol of man's control, kills Tiamet, the dragon goddess of Chaos. This is the same earth dragon spirit that represents the organized forces of nature in many early belief systems from Chinese to pagan. Though many tribal and pagan religions since then have recognized a more holistic partnership with the earth, most of the world's diverse major religions and cultures have viewed earth as something over which they claim domain and ownership rights. The legend of St. George killing the dragon (symbol of the chaotically unpredictable energy of the earth), is simply a continuation of the misguided affirmation, which took root just four thousand years ago; that mankind is able to control the chaos and shape culture by force, according to his own preconceived order. As we will see, the power of chaos that we naturally harness to change our world is demonstrated in virtually all of the achievements of civilization and technology that we treasure. Yet where the chaos is determinedly forced by us, as would-be masters of the earth, the resultant product usually creates more misery for our species.

The discoveries of chaos theory have firmly removed the basis for centuries of deterministic thinking both in science and in government. The societies that we form in this world can no longer be viewed as if they were giant and very complicated machines that need a control structure of ever increasing complexity in order to be successfully managed. The secret of nature's most complex structures is in the simple techniques by which they are built and managed, combining a simple repetitive act with the strangely helpful chaos of unpredictability, in order to make their growth and evolution in this world successful. The networks of nature consist of an infinite number of components acting as feedback loops into the whole. Each component is constantly feeding information and activity into the system and modulating its own behaviour according to the whole system's activity.

This new science of chaos has a more holistic view of the world and a recognition of the apparently universal tendency of complex systems to create order within themselves - to exhibit what is termed "self-organization." The capacity of the world to create harmony on its own, to create a pattern within a multitude of events, is one that has been glimpsed by mystics, artists and assorted individuals from time immemorial. Scientists now recognise it too, and in the next century the importance of these new discoveries will eclipse even those of relativity and quantum mechanics. Scientists can now witness this harmony of self-organization and recreate it using fractal geometry on a computer -

which led to these mathematical fractals being dubbed the "Thumbprint of God."

The mathematical fractal discoveries were a by-product of mathematician Benoit Mandelbrot's determination to discover the geometry of the repetitive patterns that he recognized in nature. Often for the first time, this fractal mathematics gave scientists in other fields the tools they needed to look at the patterns and forms of their subjects. Mandelbrot was frustrated by the inability of Euclidean geometry to measure natural forms like mountains, clouds and trees. They are made up neither of circles, rectangles, triangles nor straight lines, yet the Latin roots of "geo-metry" mean "measurement of the earth." Mandelbrot has a particularly perceptive pair of eyes and he enjoys using them and acknowledging their inputs. This is not a very "scientific" thing to do other than for data recording. His eyes could see the repetitive geometry that made up a tree, a bank of clouds or a range or mountains. He saw the formula of the clouds before he was able to mathematically describe it with numbers and letters.

It was after he started work on the fractal geometry of nature that he was led to further research of the near-abandoned work of two unusual French mathematicians from 1918-1919 (Julia and Fatou). He studied the non-linear formulae they worked with and, in an attempt to map them out, discovered (in 1980) the now famous Mandelbrot set - the strangest beast ever found through mathematics. When you understand fractals you understand that they are no more computer generated than is a photograph generated by a camera. The Mandelbrot set and other fractals exist through the repeatable but unexpected, unpredictable and inexplicable organization of points on a piece of paper. The computer simply enables us to see a representation of how these individual points* have behaved when struck with a formula. In much the same way a camera will show us how each light beam behaved when it touched the identical grains of film. Neither the computer nor the formula actually create the fractal image. It is done by the process of iteration, of repeating the same process over and over with a very slight modification each time it is done. That same powerful process is the key to meditation, to chanting of mantras or Hail Marys and to the pure fractal images that can be derived through constant feedback to a video camera of its own starting image.

*The points are simply those points on the page or computer screen, which have been assigned the value of the co-ordinates of their location on the x,y graph of that page.

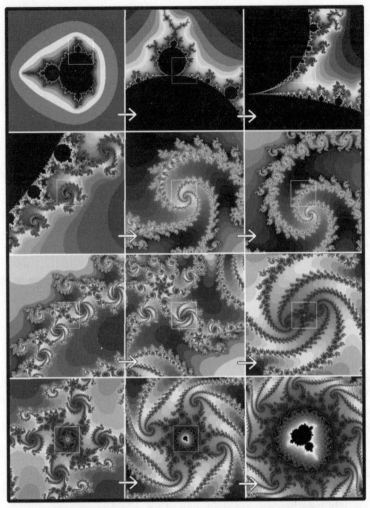

Zoom into the Mandelbrot set, final frame magnification is 17.6 trillion.

Scientists now recognize patterns of self-organization in far more exciting areas than the dots on a blank computer screen. They are becoming aware of a universe composed of interlinking sub and super-levels of organization such as that which exists within the random neural network of our own brains and within the self-regulating phenomena that keep this earth's atmosphere within those very narrow and seemingly precarious parameters necessary for life. James Lovelock was the first scientist to recognize our earth itself as a whole living organism, consisting of an infinity of interconnected components.

One of the other great discoveries of chaos theory is that called "sensitive dependence on initial conditions." This is commonly known as the "Butterfly Effect," the recognition by Edward Lorenz that something as insignificant as a butterfly flapping its wings in, say, Ecuador could make the difference between a rainstorm or a hurricane many months later and thousands of miles away. The "initial" in "initial conditions" is any point in time and space you choose. Future generations may find it hard to comprehend the arrogance of our scientific cultural base that was set to be turned around in 1961 when Edward Lorenz took a numeric short-cut that led him to an unexpected new destination.

That serendipitous diversion triggered the discovery that in a non-linear system simulating the weather, a seemingly insignificant change in local wind speed (say of one thousandth of a m.p.h. in an area of one square inch) equivalent to that caused by a passing butterfly's wing flap will, some months or years down the weather system, result in a completely different outcome to the total system. The butterfly didn't actually cause or trigger anything. The discovery was that the most seemingly insignificant event can have a profound effect in shaping the outcome of the future.

If the significance of this seems hard to swallow, let me give you a much easier example. There are many in your own life that you will recall and many more that you do not even recognise. Something as insignificant as a pause to pass wind can make you miss a bus, whereby you meet someone at the bus stop and strike up a conversation - the script can go anywhere from here but that conversation could change your career, get you married or just trigger you to go see a movie which will change in subtle ways your reactions and relationships with the world thereafter. Every input and output, however insignificant, affects not only your life but also the future of the world in some small way, and often quite dramatically in a seemingly unrelated way.

The butterfly of chaos theory has made a nonsense of all the linear projections of politicians, economists and their ilk. In today's ever more complex world, that which changes history is rarely predicted - the great crash of 1929, the collapse of the Berlin Wall, the Gulf War, Mad Cow Disease. Even in the aftermath of these events, there is rarely any perception of the eventual changes and consequences of the event.

On more mundane matters, as well, the forecasts and projections are regularly completely out of touch with the actual reality, whether we are looking at weather or economic statistics. What chaos theory

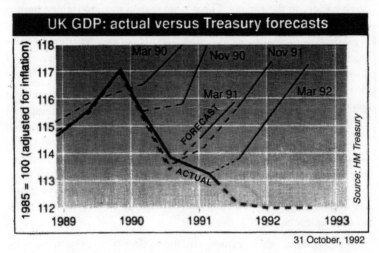

UK GDP: actual versus Treasury forecasts

Source: HM Treasury

31 October, 1992

proves, which may now seem self-evident to you, is that even if the weather forecasters had one million "non-invasive" data inputs per cubic millimetre of planet earth, accurate to a hundred decimal places, they would still not be able to forecast exactly when it might rain in a few days time. All they can hope for is that it all goes as it has in previous years, following established trends and averages. Hurricane? What hurricane? Mad Cows? We're perfectly sane!

Science has, for many years, worked on the principle that if you had enough data available you would be able to get the weather absolutely right. In the late 1950's it was readily believed that, as we increased our knowledge of weather systems and our chemical and technical ability, we would ultimately gain some rudimentary control over the weather of the world. The ingrained principle of determinism which led to such fanciful thinking has now been firmly overturned in the world of science.

The state has, for many years, been firmly run on the equally unsupportable principle that with enough data and sufficient force applied in the right places, it can not only accurately predict the course of society, but actually direct and manipulate it at will. We now are faced with the evidence that it is not possible to achieve this objective through the forcing of some parts of a complex system and have centuries of experience of the state's manipulations going wrong. Yet many of us still hang onto the hope that some day they will find a way to successfully shape society to their plans. There is no reason to suppose that human society, alone in the universe, is somehow exempt from the rules that govern the development of complex systems.

> *"Every time the government attempts to handle our affairs, it costs more and the results are worse than if we had handled them ourselves."*
>
> *Benjamin Constant, 1820*
> *French author and politician*

We do not get government through the hapless attempts of the state to forcibly control and shape society. We get instead a counter-evolutionary interference in the development of the self-governing structures that our complex society would otherwise produce. This process is always *at* our cost and usually *to* our cost, that is to say we pay the bills and we suffer the consequences.

Many of these self-governing structures already do exist in our society and flow so smoothly that we do not even recognize them. Like the fractal patterns of the natural world, our own society has an invisible order and pattern to it that is not superimposed from above, but created by a network of freely operating interdependent systems. Many of these self-governing structures have been developed over the course of many generations, changing and adapting to a changing society. Whilst the components of these structures may be subject to some forced interface with the state (see The State of Business) the pattern of this system is largely self-organized.

We are not aware, nor have we needed to be, of the invisible structure that combines to feed a large city on a daily basis, nor of the multilayered systems that permeate our society to ensure that we are clothed, fed, read, entertained and usually able to find a hot drink at a cafe somewhere not too far from our home. When the state directs things we call it government, but when we let it happen by itself with no fuss or mess we don't call it anything. We do not even see a problem when we already have the solution in place. Chaos theory now recognizes the patterns that evolve in complex systems. Chaos theory shows us how the severed feedback loop between the state and its "clientele" prevents the state from actually governing society. Instead of governing society, the state seeks to dictate and enforce the conditions that it thinks to be "best" for society in some general sense.

5. Playing God?

When we accuse someone of "playing God," it is usually because of their forced intervention into events in order to achieve some kind of perfect plan they seek to execute. Well, this just isn't how God goes about things, though you could be forgiven for suspecting that some of the wonders of the world were planned in detail by a divine being.

The universe and everything in it was quite evidently not planned by somebody kind of like us but one heck of a lot smarter - God sitting at the Universal Computer plotting out all those microbes, molecules and chromosomes - making wood soft and iron hard, deciding where the mountains and deserts go, whether you catch your bus or not, and when your third baby tooth is due. If you were God, wouldn't you have better things to do? Wouldn't you build some handy labour-saving device into your system so you could chill-out sometimes and conceive new universes?

God, however you wish to perceive It, created a universe in which everything was free to create its own future. God does not work to a predetermined plan, but the Universe itself creates an order from the events that take place within it. The understanding of this in the new science of chaos theory shows us that when you have a large number of seemingly unconnected events flowing freely, they are much more likely to form relationships, a flowing stability and order than some mish-mash of mixed-up tangled relationships that don't work. This looks like a bona-fide universal rule, yet for a long time humankind has worked on the principle that order must be deterministically shaped from the chaos; order and stability created according to either our plan or our linear interpretation of God's plan. Today's mainstream God of Christianity and Islam is often perceived to have planned our world, and dictated down to specifics how we should behave.

Of course, it is the failure of these plans, God-given or man-made that is the most frequent cause of grief to our species. For reasons that we all innately understand, our reaction to the death of 1500 from an earthquake in Italy is dwarfed by the horrible shelling of 70 cafe-goers in the centre of Sarajevo or the bombing of a dancehall in Northern Ireland. We live on the earth and must accept that it has a destiny of its own that may or may not fit in with our city-siting plans and personal lifetime goals. But the cold technological killing of each other for the benefit of the eventually successful tax-collector, whether church, state, or terrorist seeking to be tomorrow's ruler, is so obviously not part of God's way that we shudder at a more visceral level.

Putting our trust in God and loving God are at the earliest core of many religious teachings, combined with the overall rule of showing consideration to others. Yet by the time this trust and love are filtered through central control they become obedience to the church's instructions and fear of the Lord should you disobey them. The great prophets sought to share their wisdom with us so that we might better pursue the path of being fulfilled and happy human beings. They sought to give us principles and thought tools, not preachers and rules.

God's power is based on allowing every element of creation to be free to create and enjoy its own destiny, in a universe which is somehow programmed to create order. We enjoy this order in everything from the delicate skin of our earth's atmosphere to the complex set of bacteria that protect our own skin and help us digest our food. This free system works, and when we use our considerable intellectual powers to construct an artificial structure that attempts to forcibly control the system, we are not playing at being God - we are denying and obstructing the greatest tool that God built into the universe.

6. Can You Believe It?

Wherever you may be on the planet, the political power holders are almost certainly telling you that everything is going to be all right as long as they get to keep holding the controls. They will be taking credit for anything that is functioning well in society and putting blame elsewhere for whatever is going wrong. Of course, they are sure that their policies and programmes will soon bring about full employment, a roof over every head, honest and responsible politicians and public servants, improved health, reduced taxation and less crime on our streets.

Do you believe them? Do you truly believe that the problems facing society will be sorted out when the right man or party gets into power, and that some new rearrangement of the controls will properly "tune" the economic climate and bring about all the benefits promised by that man or party? Or do you, like most people interested in the process, think primarily in terms of which party or person is the lesser evil, sometimes even overriding that simple logic in order to punish the party that is currently IN power.

You should think about these questions more deeply than you are accustomed to, since, if you are the average citizen of a "developed" nation, **about half of your working life and productivity*** is devoted to supporting the proposition that some day the state will get it all miraculously right, will cease being a burden on the back of society and will become a true servant of our society, rather than a Frankensteintype creation to be milked by politicians, manipulated by special interest groups, lobbied by big business and courted for supplies by war makers around the world, to mention but a few of its major functions.

* Total taxation on the wealth society creates in any given year ranges from 40-60% in most developed countries, and has done nothing but grow since the start of this century. Add up the import duties, excise taxes (petrol, tobacco, alcohol, etc.), National Insurance, income tax, corporation tax, Value Added Tax, business rates, council tax , capital gains tax, death duties - they all come out of society's pockets one way or another. For the several centuries prior to World War 1 this total taxation was closer to the 10% mark.

Do not believe them. The larger any state becomes the greater a burden it becomes to society as a whole. It used to be less common for both partners in a relationship to need wage-earning jobs when taxation was half or less today's level. The evidence indicates that the more money the state spends on any particular problem, the worse it is likely to become over the long term. The more determined the efforts they make to control crime and disorder, the more holes appear in the moral fabric of society. When so much of our behaviour is legislated, we can easily forget the meaning of personal responsibility and risk confusing morality with sticking to the regulations. Stringent controls applied to force one element of the economic structure into "control" usually create worse ramifications in other elements of that complex structure. And the ultimate solution, the totalitarian state, creates a mirror image of order through absolute control whilst building up the steam for an eventual collapse or explosion into gross disorder.

> *"That government is best which governs least, because its people discipline themselves."*
>
> *Thomas Jefferson*

7. Natural Government vs state control

Without the state, who will run the emergency services, educate our children, set speed limits and so forth? This is the first thought that usually springs to mind. The former rulers of the Soviet Union and the current rulers of China cannot imagine how a nation could feed itself without the state regulating the situation. For seven years after the end of World War II, Britain maintained food rationing because its rulers had become so used to it, that they could not believe such a complex and important function to society would be able to somehow self-organize all on its own. They have a point - it seems that only chaos theory can explain the miracle of how all the interacting factors in cities the size of London, Bombay, New York or Mexico City conspire to feed all of the inhabitants according to their own tastes and means on a daily basis without any central organisation or planning. It is government from the bottom up, led by the . Though we rarely recognize or acknowledge the invisible natural government that arises in a free food chain, it keeps our larders filled with whatever we desire.

And this miraculous stuff isn't just happening in the food industry. Though SOME elements of our society have been regulated and run by a state of some sort or another for more than a few centuries, MOST of that which we rely upon is actually largely out of their hands and working very well. We can take many things for granted from our own natural government. Look around, examine your own life and ask what it is that you can rely on from the progress of society. As well as being able to regularly feed yourself, you are probably able to be clothed, furnish your home, buy materials with which to communicate, sell and trade your skills, read literature, make phone calls, travel from place to place, watch TV or video, work-play with a computer, insure against the risks of life, listen to music, party and do many of the other things we associate with living our lives. NONE OF THESE products or activities were conceived or initially developed by any state - they, together with almost everything we can depend upon with some reliability, emerged from the chaotic interaction of a society made up of many millions of freely acting human beings. The patterns that arise from this chaotic exchange form most of the fabric of our daily lives, and are governed from the bottom up, by the people. It is democracy without the demagogues.

Even a highly complex structure like the international airline industry started off with just two bicycle mechanics pursuing a personal dream. The Wright brothers could never in their wildest dreams have envisioned the scale of the industry that was to follow the invention of their flying machine, nor imagine its effect upon our mobility as a civilisation. Most of this complex industry evolved over the past 90 years from the chaos of our changing culture. No government directive created the package holiday, the bucket shop, or decreed that by the year 1990 we would be able to cross the Atlantic in eight hours for £100, with a vegetarian meal option. It was neither planned nor implemented by a central body using deterministic techniques.* As a result, aeroplane travel has become less expensive, safer and easier to use during these ninety years.**

* One <u>unplanned</u> spin-off of World War II was a glut of trained pilots and cheap aeroplanes which provided a big boost to the airline industry.

** Our biggest fear, and a major inconvenience to travel, is caused by aeroplanes having been drawn into the battlefield between the state and those seeking to unseat or rearrange it with coercion - today's terrorists. We do not often worry about robbers or criminals having a go at the airline industry.

If you search through history for beneficial contributions to society that had their origins in state planning or state programmes, you will find a frugal harvest - things like margarine, radar and fondue.* Do not give the state credit for the progress and order that society created, often after having to overcome the resistance and regulations of the state. The state views most radical changes to the established order as a threat to its existence and still bans or strictly controls possession of computers and communication technology in much of the world. Increasingly, the Western states can be seen to grasp at a greater control of the form and content of the Internet.

> **INDEPENDENT** june 1992
>
> # Brussels threatens organic farming

*The Swiss national dish, developed to deal with a cheese surplus.

Though the state created the original Internet structure as a means of surviving a Russian missile strike at any one computer base, it was society that created the Internet of today, which is fast dissolving the redlines of national boundaries through global communication. This was never something that was intended by the state to happen, and we must now hope that the Internet is as resistant to legislative attack by the state as it would be to a nuclear missile strike. In over-ruling an attempt in 1996 by the U.S. state to control the Internet, Judge Stewart Dazell stated: "Just as the strength of the Internet is Chaos, so the strength of our liberty depends upon the chaos and cacophony of the unfettered speech the First Amendment protects."

The state's governing record on issues of safety and pollution often lags far behind the public awareness that would otherwise prompt corporate and evolutionary change. For decades we have watched the state stifle damning evidence on asbestos, nuclear accidents and pesticide poisoning, and still (11 years on) we are assured that British beef is safe and that nuclear power is economic and manageable. The state is most often to be seen harassing, silencing and even imprisoning those pioneers who seek to raise public awareness of these issues, be they research scientists with unwelcome findings, organizations such as Greenpeace or individuals who wish to express their protest with a freewheeling DIY lifestyle. Their legislation usually follows the change that society is already implementing. Even slavery was already out of practice in half of the United States and most of Europe when President Lincoln waged war on his neighbours in the South, not because they practised slavery, but because they sought to dissolve the common union which had been agreed upon eighty years earlier. Only later in the war did the abolition of slavery became an official cause - to rally moral support and ensure God was on the right side. If 60% of businesses rely upon slaves or child-labourers, there is no climate for any state to ban it. Even today, revelations about prison labour in China or child labour in India come from consumer groups, not our national governments. Consumers can stop it quite effectively if they wish to and have prompted such change throughout history, often without even being aware of the process.

Because of the state's often inadequate setting of "minimum safe" levels for various toxins that are placed into our food and environment we also lose the ability to obtain justice from the original creators of these products when they are subsequently found to have damaged our lives. Because Company X kept to the government standards they do not have to be responsible for the damage their products create. This must, one suspects, lead to less consideration for those long-term consequences when the products are initially introduced, or when the first awareness comes that there may be damaging consequences to their use. In some cases it also leads to heavy lobbying by Company X to persuade the government to overlook negative research about, for instance, some low-calorie sweetener they seek to introduce, thereby giving the product state approval and themselves freedom from liability. The climate is perfect for a "What can we get away with" approach to moral responsibility.

The cost of financing the state's so-called governing service is immeasurably enormous and represents an added-on cost to almost everything we use in life beyond taking our breath. Be assured that all those things which are given to us "free" from the state are costing us far more as a society than if we were responsible for providing them ourselves. The misrepresentation of health services as being free, in particular, breaks the customer and service-provider relationship that we should have with our doctors, and risks turning them into a near priesthood to the sick and infirm. Many of these sick, meanwhile, have been disempowered to the degree that they no longer feel responsible even for something as basic as their own health. It also makes the "service" highly expensive and creates the controlled market in which drug companies can charge the extortionate prices that include the cost of manipulating and massaging the system.

In addition to the multiple layers of taxation we have the expensive and wasted effort of trying to live under the attack of the state. When things are "normal," we suffer the constant "requirements" of the state that increase our workload: the need to maintain things like VAT records if trying to run a business, to supply statistics to government,* the submissions for permissions that often prove confrontational, extortionate fines for minor victimless offences and so forth. So many of our interfaces with the state are confrontational rather than cooperative. On the world view we also have the costs of rebuilding bombed cities and infrastructures, maintaining our maimed and wounded, supporting the homeless refugees, the orphans and feeding the starving victims of famines that are nearly always caused by the activities of war. Yet we continue to accept this as the price we have to pay for government, oblivious to the naturally arising and reliable patterns that govern so much of our society already.

---

*It was recently estimated by that the cost to the American economy of tax collection, the actual form-filling, filing, computation, auditing etc. was between 5% and 10% of national income - close to the annual tax revenue of a century ago. *For Good and Evil: The Impact of Taxation on the Course of Civilization.*

We do not have the freedom or finances to govern ourselves under the constant burden of the state. Without this burden, and with the consequent release of wealth back to society, it is neither naive nor idealistic to expect that the problems we rely on the state to manage would be greatly reduced. Products and services would become cheaper, we would have more funds to deal intelligently with our remaining problems, and there would be a considerable boost in positive enterprise and employment as society rose to meet the challenge of providing those services that the state has been mismanaging for decades and in some cases centuries.

We must not allow ourselves to fall into the despair-lined trap of assuming that something is not possible because it has never been done. A great teacher of mine assisted me over this hurdle when he made two salient points about the Wright Brothers invention of the aeroplane - points that could apply to most of the major discoveries that have advanced our civilisation.

1) Was it impossible to fly before the Wright brothers invented the aeroplane?

2) The Wright brothers did not invent flight by fighting falling.

The answer to the first question is of course no - it was possible to fly but nobody had yet figured out how. The point that my teacher (Professor Galambos) was making is that FREEDOM IS POSSIBLE even though it may not have existed in our recent evolution.*

*A successful free society did thrive like nowhere else in Medieval Europe for over a century at Ditmarschen, on land that farmers had reclaimed from the sea. It prospered without coercive control and taxes, until taken over in 1559 with a savage massacre of civilians by the Duke of Holstein's cavalry. (Author note: some of my ancestors came from Ditmarschen)

What we can learn from the second point is that we do not successfully build something by attacking its opposite. You may notice that groups and bodies who set out to "fight" something or launch a "war" on it are rarely successful in their aims, though they may spend vast sums of money and receive much publicity in the course of it. We will not succeed by attacking or fighting the state with variations of its own coercive tools. We can succeed by discovering ways to stop, discourage and dis-empower the state's interference with our own evolution towards more permanent, effective and efficient natural government with no need for "central control."

"It is organized violence at the top which creates individual violence at the bottom."

Emma Goldman

8.   Legitimising Coercion

One of the great crimes of the state is that it has eroded our own natural repulsion to coercion as an acceptable behaviour mode for society. The legitimisation of coercion at the so-called top, because it is deemed necessary for the good of the people (that is, for the good of the state) percolates down throughout a society which looks to leaders "in charge of things" for a value system.

Let's face it - most of us are naturally repelled by coercive behaviour, by people threatening to hit us or damage us if we don't do what they want. And most of us also are programmed by our own society's culture, and perhaps by our own instincts, **not to do** things in this way. We prefer to request, purchase, trade, suggest or argue as our means to inter-relate with the rest of society. The ultimate act of coercion is that of killing another person and this, not coincidentally, is one of the

> *"The direct use of force is such a poor solution to any problem, it is generally employed only by small children and large nations."*
>
> *David Friedman:*

most universal natural taboos found in different societies across the world. People are not the killers of the world. It is the organized and rigid belief systems of the world which convince us that their righteous cause is greater than the value of our individual lives. The greatest tragedies of human history have been wreaked upon us by priests, leaders, politicians and nation states, not from the odd murderer arising out of ordinary society and killing a few people - or even a lot of people - before being caught. And it is likely that the majority of those killers who do arise in society received their initial training in a government uniform.

For the higher purposes of the state, coercion is now alright, and all of their instructions to us are backed by the threat to hit or damage us if we do not comply. Coercion is the basic stick of the state. Almost nothing the state does could be done without it. Let's take a quick trip through coercion and consider the consequences of its use in society. "To coerce" is described by Collins dictionary as "to compel or restrain by force or authority without regard to individual wishes or desires." The lion does not coerce the wildebeest into being his dinner - he just kills it and eats it. How does the state use coercion on us? Using a simple example like a parking fine, let us say that you absolutely refuse to pay this ticket or spend time in the court process trying to prove, say, that the police had blocked your return due to a bomb scare. Anyway, no way are you going to pay sixty pounds, dollars or whatever to this uncaring and unresponsive state-sanctioned agency. Neither will you run and hide, accept losing your freedom and going to jail, or let anyone impound your car or in any way let them get your money. So what do they do? They will get your money, and they will coerce you into paying it; and assuming that you are a relatively sane person, you will abandon your determination and pay them.

Why? Because coercion ultimately means that if you are not willing to pay the fine or go to jail or run away you can be killed. Shocking isn't it? Of course they have bailiffs and ways of seizing your sixty whatevers before it comes to this; but if you really did not want them to get their fine money and had made it inaccessible or burnt it, then they would come to put you in prison. If you sought to successfully resist this, without going into hiding, then such a position would almost certainly end in your own death were the full force of the law applied, or they would get you into jail after all, but alive.

This is a simple example and an extreme case. Only a nutter would throw away his or her life over such a small thing. But that is what coercion is - in its rawest purest form coercion is the province of the armed forces, who make no bones about the principle that *might is right*. When a soldier or a mugger points a gun at you, you do what you are told and you both know it is because the gun is there, and not because you voted for him, or that he has the better logic or God on his side.

Many crimes involve coercion: when your property is stolen, or you are mugged, conned, or passed counterfeit money. Just about any crime with a victim has involved coercion. It seems reasonable that society should be able to use coercion back to capture and punish the criminals, if necessary forcing them physically to cease and desist their activities, maybe even killing them if they have killed. Organized coercion against these criminals by a police force may well be a moral and reasonable approach and may well work as a deterrent, but that does not mean that there are not better and more effective methods to deal with crime and its victims - methods that rely less, or not at all, on the use of coercion. I do not suggest that none of these methods exist today, but that many more would have evolved, had the state not claimed a virtual monopoly on defining crime and dealing with it for so long.

Our whole culture is permeated with coercively backed laws and regulations that do not in fact protect anyone from the dangers described above. Here coercion is used to make us drive safely, build according to council wishes, register new-born children with the state and many other simple things. Coercion and disregard for personal liberty are the essence of the tax-collecting laws. Despite all the laws that supposedly protect us from crime, only the tax collecting laws were strong enough to arrest Al Capone, the clever and arrogant gangster of America's early Mafia. What does this tell us of the state's priority?

Even on the level of a small nuclear family or an extended clan, the constant imprint from the state that purports to govern us all, is that coercive techniques are alright when special interests, including that of the "common good," are at stake. Parents may well come to regard their families as mini-states, to be run accordingly with punishments and much use of coercive "training." I am not objecting to or directing how families should raise children, since experimentation here is a part of the evolutionary process and parents have near total power over their children in the fundamentally important early stages of their lives. Because the universe tends to create successful organisms we have a good basic programming and most of us would naturally shrink from using coercive techniques when infants and children are involved. This is why kids around the world get away with a lot more than adults.

However, taking their example from the state, many parents will either overcome or ignore their inner programming and force and threaten and sometimes beat their children into submission "for their own good." Though we may not be trained psychologists most of us know the results of this approach. We can take encouragement from the many instances where individuals have been able to overcome, learn and grow stronger after exposure to some pretty nasty treatment.

Because coercion - forcing people to do things - is so much at the core of the state structuring of society it becomes easier for the petty or the highly organised thief to rationalise his or her actions by comparing them to the morality of the state and recognising that even greater crimes are being committed by those who are called leaders but are in fact self-interested rulers. When the Mafia demands protection money from a restaurant they are doing just what the taxman does, and may in some cases be giving better service for it and demanding less. When a lawbreaker bribes a policeman, as can happen all over the world, they acknowledge that they both operate within the same flawed moral framework. When a businessman bribes a politician in order to generate preferential the competition, they are being enticed into dishonesty by the coercive facilities of the state. Waste, corruption and inefficiency on many levels continually permeate state and state related activities - **what does this tell us about the mechanism they are using?**

Coercion is, simply, the big divide. With it as the basic enforcing mechanism, society's natural evolution is warped and distorted. Coercion disregards the feedback loop. The state cannot survive without coercion and we cannot successfully evolve with it. As bad as big business can sometimes be, it does not use the coercive mechanism UNLESS it is using the state as its agent.* The basic remit of any business, big or small, is to perceive and deliver products to us that we want. If they spend money seeking to convince us we want that product, then so be it - that money goes into society's pockets too and is ultimately redistributed among us. It pays for most of our newspapers, TV and radio. If we pay for a product from business and it is a bummer we are not coerced into buying it again next week and the month after and the year after that until, at election time, we get the big opportunity to choose another supplier for that same product that we do not want.

*Unfortunately, an increasing number of corporations do get involved in the processes of the state. See Chapter 22: The State of Business.

We must recognise that coercion is not a viable mechanism for change. In the long term it always produces negative results. That we think coercion to be a traditional and natural way to run the world of "men" is a frightening situation. The ingrained and often gratuitous use of coercion by states around the world has, simply, made it easier for individuals to rationalise away their own violent or oppressive behaviour and overcome many of the natural strictures that evolution and society would otherwise place upon us. This is why we must not, in our minds, legitimise coercive behaviour as acceptable despite the fact that our so-called leaders use it as their stock-in-trade. Look into history and see where it got them.

> *"The end move in politics is always to pick up a gun."*
>
> *Buckminster Fuller (1895 - 1983)*

An apt and true reply was given to Alexander the Great by a pirate who had been seized. For when that king had asked the man what he meant by keeping hostile possession of the sea, he answered with bold pride. "What thou meanest by seizing the whole earth; but because I do it with a petty ship, I am called a robber, whilst thou who dost it with a great fleet art styled emperor."

St. Augustine, The City of God (354 - 430 A.D.)

The "you are being watched" sign attending the UK's tens of thousands of cameras mounted on roads around the country. Such notices to not attend the CCTV's all over the country, which are there to gather information on us rather than prompt fear.

9. The Constant Confrontation

Whoever is in power got there because they fought their way there. Those who hold some of the reins may change from time to time but the power structure, the state, remains in place. This structure in which they thrive was originally brought into existence by booting out a previous power structure or even an entire race. There are very few instances in history where power has been willingly relinquished - without a fight. Doddering old men grip determinedly to the reins of power until they are struck down either by disease, palace revolt or coup. The most unpopular regimes continue to exert their will upon a populace when all vestiges of satisfaction or support have gone - holding on until the final humiliation of being trapped in their office, bunker, bedroom or even the back of a truck - and then being either shot, hung from a lamppost or processed through the courts they once controlled, and exposed to the contempt of a public whom they once thought to be "their people." The so-called democracy we enjoy today is but a thin veneer over the basic mechanics of the state, and those mechanics have always hinged on the lever of confrontation.

> *"It is safe to assert that no government proper ever had a provision in its organic law for its own termination"*
>
> *ABRAHAM LINCOLN,*
> *Inaugural address 1861*

The handful of parties claiming to represent our best interests are all locked in constant confrontation, only sleeping with each other in the interests of defeating a common enemy. Almost everything you read of the politics of the state is the story of a confrontation between two groups, usually bitterly opposed to each other. Should the government of the day "lose" a vote then it is deemed that they are getting weak and unable to manage the country. This state of confrontation is thought to be (and is accepted as) the normal way of doing business for the state. And even though the state is ostensibly there to "serve" us, the most usual experience that most of us, law-abiding and otherwise, have is that of confrontation; whether over building permits, parking tickets, tax demands or any other confrontation prompted by the state's desire that we all fit perfectly with the fine-tuning of their plan for society.

I do not mean to suggest that society should have no plan or order.

When large groups of people live together and share resources, they have always developed accepted modes of behaviour as a social group, and use different techniques to encourage the acceptance of these modes amongst a greater society. These methods have undoubtedly re-

---

Judge jails woman driver

A FEMALE judge in Los Angeles has jailed a mother for causing the death of her infant son in a car crash because she had not put the child's seat belt on.

Lesia Pappas, aged 33, sobbed as Judge Shari Silver sentenced her to the maximum 18 months for vehicular manslaughter in the

Nov, 1996   *Christopher Reed, Los Angeles*

---

lied upon state involvement for a long time, but for many previous cultures the threat of rejection by the community has been a greater tempering agent upon behaviour than fear of being locked up or fined. The police, as a force on the streets, only developed in most parts of the world towards the end of the last century. The numbers in prison per 1000 just a few generations ago were a fraction of those incarcerated today, and the main reason for the increase lies in the rapid growth of laws against behaviour or activities that have no actual victim (see Chapter 18: Victimless Crimes). I would be curious to know if history has ever recorded our legislators projected a need for fewer prisons as a result of their new crime policies.

As mentioned elsewhere herein, our development of self-governing techniques within society has eroded over the generations in which the state has assumed more and more legislative responsibility for our morals and behaviour. Many would like to believe that the state can take care of everything from their health and social security to their food purity and air standard. In practice, the state has not done a good long-term job of any of this, and indeed has often obstructed efforts to improve them by suppressing reports, silencing scientists and subsidizing polluters and land-clearance programs.

Look at what we have evolved without confrontation but by ourselves - human to human. We have music from classical to techno, with jazz, rock, beep bop and whatever you like in between. You can buy any, all or none of them - one has not had to supplant the other, even though they may "battle it out" in the marketplace. Though we can choose from wholewheat bread, white bread, French bread, naturally leavened bread, rye bread, rolls, buns, croissants and many other forms of flour and water to have with our meal, most in this country have chosen the sliced white loaf, for better or worse. In India the same options are possible in a city such as Bombay, but the over-riding choice is chapati, paratha or puri. Or, you can choose rice instead. There is no need in society for one choice or decision to confront and beat all the others as some separate process. However, in the affairs of the state this is the basic mechanism at play, one group opposing another in each decision-making process - unless some compromise is reached whereby we all have slightly brown bread sliced half way through the loaf. The state specializes in making decisions of an EITHER/OR nature whereas in society we manage much more successfully with a BOTH/AND* policy, allowing individual decision-making to play the major part in shaping order. When I visited East Berlin, just before it rejoined its other half, the results of these different approaches were apparent in the comparative restaurant menus on offer.

*It was the strategic embrace of the BOTH/AND philosophy that was one of the keys to the success of the user-friendly Apple Macintosh against the rigidly linear operating system of IBM.

We may have grievances and problems with existing aspects of our culture whether they relate to racial awareness, attitudes to the disabled, male domination, dangerous drug usage or corporate irresponsibility. But we cannot successfully deal with these problems by enlisting the support of the state in a confrontational attack on them. We need only look at the success they have had in their fight against crime, homelessness, or in the war on drugs.

As we now understand from chaos theory and the study of complex systems, the systems which are both stable and flexible are those which co-operate with other systems through an intricate and self-organized network. Co-operation, interdependence, freedom and flexibility are the key elements to any successful harmonious system and they are all notably absent in the confrontational activities of the state.

IN another small blast of the trumpet against bureaucratic verbosity, this list, issued without comment, is circulating around Government departments in Washington . . .

56 words	Lord's Prayer:
118 words	23rd Psalm
226 words	Gettysburg Address
297 words	Ten Commandments
15,269 words	U.S. Dept of Agriculture Order on cabbage pricing

reported in the Daily Mail, July 1985

10.   A Terminal Toolbag

With the fundamental structure of the state founded upon the belief that determinism is able to control a complex system, it is no surprise to discover that the basic mechanisms and tools upon which the state relies are fatally flawed in their construction. Here are just a few examples.

THE OVERGROWTH MECHANISM - State structures usually have no mechanism that adjusts their size to the needs of the occasion. So they overgrow if enough money is available. It would seem to be a natural desire of most forms of organisation to grow and prosper. If not enough money is available after society has been taxed to its limit, the state can and does print more to cover budget overrun, thus providing the basic fuel of inflation.

Companies classically grow bigger by supplying more product to their customers. They have their faults, sometimes selling crap products, cheating to gain competitive advantage or spending more on advertising than quality maintenance. But if we stop buying a company's crap products then they do stop growing and actually can become smaller - and eventually even cease to exist.

The state grows bigger by simply deciding we need its services to "manage" an ever increasing number of the perceived needs of society - needs that it perceives with the supposed mandate of the people given by voting - more about that later. Most of what the state now "manages" at great cost, was not an area of its control or responsibility less than one century ago. The state spends much of its time just looking for new things to manage and control, continually passing new laws and regulations, with little thought given to removing previous irrelevant ones. This growth of assumed responsibility and the resulting laws and regulations, seem to be checked only by the wealth-creating skills of the society on which it feeds. As long as the money is there to support it, the state will feed on this and grow in influence. In extreme cases one state will seek to grow by forcibly taking over another.

Whether state management is running the roadworks department of a local council, "social security," a police constabulary or the Ministry of Agriculture, it will always seek to advance its own growth and perceived importance and, unless restrained, will steadily and relentlessly expand. In something as simple as a local roads department in the U.K.

it is obvious that at a certain point there are basically sufficient roads in the community and the actual cost of maintaining the existing system is greatly reduced and easily managed. Rather than cut the department back though, they proceed with constant rebuilding of the existing road system for an alleged future benefit. The reality is a road system constantly clogged by rebuilding works, only a few of which relate to repair of the existing structure. Some of these works actually detract from the smooth running of a road, such as: the superfluous insertion of traffic lights at roundabouts all over the country; traffic islands that reshape themselves at regular intervals, dangerously narrowing sections of the road; the unsightly and confusing painting and repainting of lines, zig zags and grids of white and yellow; control-freak channelling of traffic into forced lanes far ahead of intersections, causing trapped motorists to wildly try and escape at the last minute; implementation of often unnecessary one-way systems; needless mini-roundabouts at otherwise well-functioning crossroads; the list goes on as new ways are constantly being sought to maintain budget and this is but one example of a local state service.

We will not dwell more on the Common Agricultural Policy here, an obvious example of unrestrained growth, other than to recognise that the massive level of fraud associated with it actually boosts its growth and creates more employment within the organisation. Fraud is not perceived as a cost by the bureaucrats who run it, even though estimates have put it at up to a third of the CAP budget, equal to billions of pounds per annum. Fraud prevention is not built into the toolbag, though it would be unimaginable to us that any of our major food companies could grow and prosper by such means.

> **Guardian - Nov 1996**
>
> **M**ORE THAN £3 billion of European Union funds is missing, according to the latest annual audit. The money, mainly destined for approved projects in member states, appears to have been misspent.
>
> Auditors calculated that funds would have been lost to agricultural fraud and cor-

THE "DISCONNECTED" FACTOR - Unlike the individual, the small company or the multinational corporation, the state does not need to ask us or even entice us in order to set its hands upon our money; neither do we have any specific say in how it is spent. There is no direct relationship between our money and the product we receive from the

state. The individual customer feedback is not considered. Thus, when we become unhappy with a service or stop using a product of the state, we must continue to pay for it and it is only if millions of others for many years are in the same position that some message may get through to the deaf supplier.

Let us look at two recent extremes to illustrate a point. When Perrier found benzene contamination in its water it recalled all stocks, lost market share and later successfully re-emerged into a much larger world market. There are many other instances of product recall and rapid damage-control exercises when problems are perceived in industry. Any large company has damage limitation plans well rehearsed for any major product problems that could occur. They recall products because they acknowledge that there has been a threat to the health of their consumers and because their insurers stipulate this.

The other example which immediately comes to mind, of course, is the British state's endless King Canute*-like stance in virtually proclaiming by decree that the virulent Mad Cow Disease did not pose a threat to the food chain. Only after that the growing trickle of young deaths threatened to become embarrassing, did they finally admit that perhaps, yes, there was a risk in allowing these diseased animals into our diet. But of course, there is no problem now, whenever "now" happens to be, and they cannot be held responsible because they listened carefully to the government scientists who said what they were paid to say.

> **Guardian - Apr 1991**
>
> ## Scientist ordered to halt 'mad cow' study
>
> **A** LEADING scientist who says he has solved the mystery of "mad cow" disease has been ordered to stop all work which would verify his claims...
>
> Dr Narang said: "All I want to do is get on with my science but barrier after barrier has been put in my way."

*King Canute knew the difference between the real laws that govern our existence on earth and the man-made laws which seek to control events with similar reliability. It was to make this point that he took his court down to the seaside and demonstrated to them that even the great and fearsome power of the king's command could not stop the tide from coming in. Perhaps he was also trying in some way to impress upon them the comparative frailty of the laws that he was being advised and urged to make. Unfortunately, it seems his point was lost and he goes down in history as some nut who thought he could command the tide. He tried to make a point but the tide of history and custom was against him.

In this second example, the British and their export customers were exposed to a fatal communicable brain disease for ten years, whilst the government dismissed the constant warnings of scientists not on their payroll. At the time of writing, Britain is virtually the only place in the world where British beef is not officially and unofficially regarded as dangerous food. British officials charged with safeguarding the public, portray the whole thing as silly foreign hysteria that us Brits with our stiff upper lips and spongy brains should not worry about. Instead we are urged to feel sorry for the poor farmers and the great British beef industry. Can you ever imagine Heinz telling us it is OK that one in a million of their famous tins of baked beans might contain a potentially fatal brain disease but we must stick by this great British product?

At least, in the case of the beef scandal, we can ignore the state's assurances and choose whether or not to consume beef, even though we still must indirectly pay for its production (and destruction). The same can not be said about areas under complete state control, such as nuclear power, policing and arms purchases, in which our personal preferences are not considered.

I do not mean to imply that companies always react as positively as did Perrier, but how often do we ever hear a government admission of some form of leak into our environment that <u>does</u> constitute a threat to human health or warrant consumer precautions. Only some thirty years after the 1957 fire at Britain's Windscale nuclear plant did we begin to learn of the true dangers to which that generation were exposed.

REPRESSION - One of the most time-honoured tools of the state is repression to silence dissent and disturbance. This sometimes works on a temporary basis but inevitably builds up to greater disorder later. Once free radio was allowed in the UK, to be "banned by the BBC" was a sure ticket to success. Repression of a small problem will often stimulate enough interest to make it a big problem. We see how the suppression of soft drugs has led to an escalating use of harder drugs.

Often strong repression also creates the classic situation where ten new converts to the "cause" spring up for every one that is knocked down (history is filled with examples, including today's breed of "eco-warriors"). Somehow when the cause is right-eous, and often when it is not, the power that is ap-plied as repression can

> *It is characteristic of the most stringent censorships that they give credibility to the opinions they attack.*
>
> *Voltaire (1694 - 1778)*

mysteriously transfer itself to those on whom it is exercised.

SUPPORT IT - We all know that when you raise or lower the price of a can of beans or a pair of boots, this will have the overall effect of either lowering or raising sales of that item. We know that if you offer more pay for a job, there will be more applicants of a generally higher calibre.

However heartless it sounds in today's climate of desperation, it is still undeniable that the more money the state pays us for being in one of the "victim" categories the more of those "victims" there will be, whether they be the unemployed, single mothers, the rent-challenged or the disabled. In a wheelchair myself, I know how often one sees the apparently able-bodied returning to cars displaying the official orange disabled badge. It may be implicit in a successful society to help real victims of circumstance to overcome hardship and misfortune whether by handouts or other more integral means as they evolve; and I maintain that the heart and intellect of humanity would be big enough if its pockets were deeper. But the state simply perpetuates the problem by paying out more and more, while having no vested interest in ever actually changing the situation that provides its bureaucrats with a living. How many examples do we have of these bodies set up to eliminate a problem, actually eliminating it, shutting down their operations and going home?

In many of the privately funded charity organisations we are now seeing an evolution towards helping victims climb out of the poverty trap by supplying wells, low-tech farming equipment, education and even sometimes a market and a fair price for their products in the West. This is the type of support that changes the situation rather than prolonging it.

Increasingly in this century, the state has taken on more of the supporting maternal role in society, always seeking to be there with a breastful of the milk of human kindness when we are in trouble; taking care of all those things that we once had to look after for ourselves when we left mother and home to become responsible adults. What the state feeds us is not milk but the polluted remnants of its own plunder from society - that which survives their own inflated salaries, palaces, wars and harebrained schemes. The money coming back has lost its meaning and its ownership - and is often expended on something other than that which was intended. It is a poisonous tit on which we suck, individuals and business alike, and in the obsession with "getting our share" of the state handout we both compromise our own integrity and trample on the true rights of others.

> Sunday Times - Jul 1997
>
> **MILLIONS** of pounds of public money have been pumped into funding dozens of British films that have never been shown in any cinema.

The state-given "right" to suck at its sorry breast is one of the basic rationales that underlines many of the regulations governing our freedom to cross red lines drawn upon the map by the world's "developed" nations . And the proffering of it too, stimulates unnatural movements of people attracted to the free lunch rather than to opportunity and change. Living without the state will mean putting some trust in the abundant milk of the great Universe that created us. This Universe is far more worthy of that trust than are the pumped up politicians constantly telling us that: "Mother knows best and father will punish us if we disagree."

ATTACK ! - A classic approach by the state to dealing with problems in our society is to set up structures to relentlessly attack them. These structures are prone to the old "unchecked growth" principle. This growth is unfortunately fed when the problem they are seeking to address becomes worse.

Thus, even an honest police force waging a genuine war on crime is subject to the principle that if they are successful they reduce their employment levels and importance. Yet if crime goes up they achieve increased importance and attract bigger budgets. I give the police the benefit of the doubt and do not suggest that they consciously encourage crime in order to build up their departments. But I must also give the organising powers of chaos and the market enough credit to realize that this inbuilt principle does not support the successful operation of the system. A clear example of this is the abundance of laws against victimless crimes, especially the drug laws, which build up unnecessary police numbers fighting an unwinna-

> Guardian Sept 1996
>
> # Jail population is soaring
>
> **T**HE jail population is rising so rapidly that a new prison is needed every three weeks, the director general of the Prison Service, Richart Tilt, warned yesterday.
>
> The 1,000-a-month increase in the prison population raised the risk of again using expensive police cells and the

ble war and diverting much needed skills from combating the crimes that involve victims. When drugs are legalised these forces will need new crimes to fight, just as the security forces at MI6 recently switched a large portion of their budget from the reduced Russian and Irish threats, instead devoting large resources to combating the newly perceived threat to liberty posed by animal rights activists and anti-road protesters in the UK.

Their are many other tools in the Toolbag, and more keep getting added as the lunacy continues. At the root of it however, the basic foundations of the state undermine its own intentions, be they good or bad. All their tools and mechanisms are built on coercion; the attempt to force things into place, which is a one-sided mechanism, divorced from the interactive principles of nature that enable a complex system to successfully develop and adapt to changing circumstances.

Guardian Nov 1997

A moral maze

Paul Brown on the 'polluter pays' dilemma at the root of an Environment Agency dispute

...The problem is that if the scales of charges are based on the level of the pollution, then the more the pollution, the greater the cash piling into the coffers of the agency.

(the Environment Agency)

The more laws and restrictions there are,
The poorer people become.
The sharper men's weapons,
The more trouble in the land.
The more ingenious and clever men are,
The more strange things happen.
The more rules and regulations,
The more thieves and robbers.

Lao Tzu, 600 B.C. - Chinese philosopher

11. Our Problems - Our Solutions

Why do we think it natural and right that the state should be the agent through which society deals with its more difficult problems, such as unemployment, bigotry, child abuse and homelessness? Their growing involvement began as a bold experiment early this century, probably with the very best of intentions, as the state began to take responsibility for society's problems. We forget that towards the end of the last century society became increasingly concerned about "social" issues; many early institutions and organizations were set up by rich industrialists with bags of money, or individuals with devotion and bags of time. The days of having bags of money, spendable locally instead of offshore, have long gone and fewer individuals have much free time, as we all scrabble to support both ourselves and the enormous machine of the state. We cannot assume that the problems of the 19th century would have remained static and unsolved had the state not become responsible for them, as we cannot know how successfully society would have evolved to deal with them. We do know that in the past eighty years, the state - putting its "terminal toolbag" to use - has spawned countless agencies to deal with the problems, as most of them have become more entrenched.

Much of our decision making, consideration, and life-planning is now bound by the assumption that the state should provide a safety net protecting us from ourselves, instead of just protecting us from those like them across the red line on the map. For many thousands of years the state was not charged with looking after many of our problems and, as far as I know, the overall levels of homelessness, unemployment, burglary, mugging, broken families, murder, assault and date-rape were lower then, and have been increasing ever since. The works of Charles Dickens and their impact upon millions of readers were probably more responsible for changing the social attitudes and practices of 19th century England than was any subsequent growth in the law and its enforcers.

The state has no God-given responsibility to look after us all, whatever may befall us. It is neither any law of nature nor a practice used by any other species on this planet. Once we accept the flawed view that being cared for by an all-powerful state is the natural order of things, we accept a severe restriction of our freedom. We end up with a hugely

expensive structure that is supposed to stop people from sleeping on
the streets, being mugged, being unemployed or taking dangerous
drugs, while itself exacerbating - if not causing - these problems. However, that which the state is supposed to prevent continues growing at a
rapid pace and this should give us pause for thought. The fact that over
70% of bankruptcies and subsequent job losses are triggered by tax col-
lectors could give us further cause to pause. One could be forgiven for
suspecting that the more money that is taken from society to spend on a
problem, the greater that problem becomes. Statistical evidence undoubtedly supports this suspicion. Big Brother does not deliver value
and the sooner we respond to this realisation the sooner will our problems begin to retreat.

These increases took place during
a DOUBLING in real terms of EXPENDITURE
on LAW and ORDER.

1000's of Notifiable Offences (England and Wales)

1978/9	1993/4	CRIME	INCREASE
544	1355	Burglary	149%
321	893	Criminal Damage	178%
118	169	Fraud and Forgery	43%
13	53	Robbery	308%
22	29	Sexual Offences	32%
1416	2852	Theft and Handling	101%
95	202	Violence against person	113%
9	39	Other offences	333%

Source: Annual Abstract of Statistics (compiled for Saturn's Children by A Duncan and D Hobson)

Society, whilst it does not have any imposed duty to look after its
poor and problematic, still makes a considerable effort through charity
and institutions to deal with many of these people. The fact that this
contribution from society continues to be substantial, despite the awful
ravages of taxation and the damage caused by the posturing and weaponry financed with it, forces one to consider the resources that society
might willingly spend on its problems in a state of freedom and re-
tained wealth.

Institutions exist to look after a vast array of problems, and people
become active even to the point of breaking the state's law in their efforts to rectify society's ailments. We find non-governmental groups
and organisations forming to support abused donkeys, war orphans,

lifeboat services, threatened woodlands, vital medical research, alcoholics, the disabled, and a myriad other areas where a member or members of society have perceived a problem and sought to forge a solution to it, starting only with the chaotic mix of their initial position. The people trying hardest, and having most success at dealing with some of the problems facing our world, are not the governments of the day but organisations started by people who saw a problem and did something about it, rather than laying back and expecting somebody else to take responsibility. Greenpeace and Reclaim the Streets are good examples, as are Amnesty and Friends of the Earth or even the Salvation Army and Boy Scouts in their day.

The state has co-opted the duty of care from society with an increasing degree of acceleration this century. Initially much of this assumption of new responsibilities was prompted by well-meaning statesmen, lobby groups and individuals seeking to ensure a greater level of care by instituting it as government policy. Whatever the initial intentions, the state is not doing a good job of it today. Whilst private agencies primarily seek to feed, clothe and protect those devastated by war, disaster or famine (most of which is caused by war) it is the governments who hand out money (our money) destined for the Swiss bank accounts of despots, or to finance nuclear power plants, or to fund environmentally damaging projects, or to purchase chemical insecticides and fertilisers, or military hardware. Usually, of course, the construction works, insecticides, or fighter jets are purchased from the country which is donating or lending the money in the first place. The list goes on as every week, in every country of the world, there are new revelations about current and past wastage and scandals involving so called "aid budgets."

Yes we need to deal with problems like homelessness, drug-addiction, pollution, malnutrition, sexual abuse, poor education, bad health and indeed the whole catalogue of society's ills. But by letting the state take responsibility for these problems we usually condemn them to ultimately becoming worse as we deprive ourselves (society) of the funds and motivation that would enable us to be more effective in finding positive and flexible solutions.

"The majority never has right on its side. Never I say! That is one of the social lies that a free, thinking man is bound to rebel against. Who makes up the majority in any given country? Is it the wise men or the fools? I think we must agree that the fools are in a terrible overwhelming majority all the wide world over."

Henrik Ibsen, dramatist (1828-1906)

"In matters of conscience, the law of the majority has no place."

Mahatma Gandhi (c 1950)

"It is not good to have a rule of many."

Homer (c 800 B.C.)

12. Voting

We are supposed to have our say on how the state "manages" our society through the democratic instrument of the vote. The word "democracy" means government by the people and not rule by a small clique running an army of bureaucrats, howsoever they are selected. Much is made of the power of the vote as an instrument giving us a fair and democratic say in how our society and government are run. Revolutions are fought for the right to vote and it was the first major objective won in the fight for equal treatment for women. It is also true though, that Adolf Hitler and many of the greatest despots of modern times were the most democratically popular when they assumed power. The vote does not give us a respite from the yoke of the state - it only provides a means to occasionally change the colour of the packaging and to do some minor tinkering with how the meagre amount of money pissed back at us gets distributed. Voting is an ingenious and well-meant attempt to translate the wishes of the people into the actions of those who

> *"The ballot box is a most inadequate mechanism for change"*
>
> *Simone de Beauvoir, 1973*

govern them. In practice, however, this rarely happens and the voting system has led to neither freedom nor true democracy wherever it is used in the world.

In the first place your vote does not give you, personally, any say whatsoever. It gives the majority a say and the majority may not have any idea of your own interests and situation. The premise that the majority is somehow "right" about a particular issue, or that there should even be issues that have to be decided in such a mechanical way, is essentially flawed. However, if we take it on board, we realise that the majority will often constitute less than one in five (20%) of the population. This is the sum you will end up with after deducting those not eligible to vote for reasons of age or nationality, those who choose not to vote at all, and those who voted for the losing parties. In some countries, such as Australia, the general apathy with the voting process reached such proportions that the state legislated mandatory voting - you must exercise your freedom to vote or risk going to jail. Presumably this law was passed with the sanction of the few remaining Australian voters at the time the legislation was introduced.

It matters not, since very few of the active voters actually vote FOR a person or party. They usually vote tactically AGAINST the other side, seeing their vote as supporting the lesser of two or more evils. Another motivation might be purely personal and based upon promised handouts to single mothers or more spending on the military, rather than the full range of policies being put forward.

In our real-world voting with the pocketbook, we drink Guinness because we prefer it, not to penalise the other brewers or put them out of business. And if enough of us become disenchanted with a product then the company producing it has either to diversify successfully or die. With the electoral vote we don't get to stop buying the product, nor do we get to buy a new product; we simply get to change the manufacturer of the product and do so on the basis of sweeping promises that they are under no actual liability to fulfil, and which in practice they seldom do.

Consider for a moment to what extent the body of the state remains constant: its volumes of regulation and law with its enforcers and interpreters; the military and defence establishment; total taxation (relentless in its rise); and the countless departments and offices filled with the vast armies of bureaucrats who run this sorry ship. Are we really to believe that even a major re-sculpture of the tip of the iceberg will make a difference to the passengers of this Titanic?

Some have suggested electronic voting, linked to your television or home computer, as the new way to better democracy - eliminating the MP's and politicians whom we love to hate. This view fails to recognise that the majority can be and frequently are manipulated. We could even have the majority of television watchers passing legislation making TV ownership

> *"Vote for the man who promises least; he'll be the least disappointing."*
>
> *Bernard Baruch, 1960*

and viewing mandatory for all citizens. Frighteningly restrictive laws could be propositioned and passed during moments of public hysteria. The concept is a severe yet ineffective tweaking of the knobs and controls of the state. Those who wish to control and direct coercive power will soon find many ways to manipulate and control the television voter.

Voting doesn't effect positive evolutionary change any more than do

armed revolutions, insurrections, invasions or fundamentalist takeo-
vers. It is simply another mechanism for determining who holds the
coercive reigns of power. Voting is freedom designed by a committee.
True freedom is far simpler and a lot more free-flowing.

As the anonymous wall graffiti reads: "Don't vote - it only encourages them." What would happen if we were somehow able to vote
against the state itself? You will find a suggestion on this in a later
chapter.

> I wanted to vote Labour but now
> I'm sick of it. I turn off party
> political broadcasts. I want
> someone to tell the truth
> **Clare Perkins, student vice-president**

A spoof London newspaper produced by Reclaim The Streets and
confiscated by the police. Did they think people would get ideas?

"When you blame others, you give up your power to change"

Dr Robert Anthony

13.   Divide and Rule

One of the silver-linings for the state provided by the new multi-party system of government is that the rulers of the day (the In Party) can always blame many of the problems facing us, upon the last party that was in power (the Out Party). Failing this, they assure us that the problem would be much worse than it already is if the Out Party were dealing with it. "Let us continue doing a bad job because the Out Party would do an even worse one." After a decade or so, kings, emperors and dynasties could not continue to use this excuse.

The flip side of this silver-lining works for the Out Party because they can always point at the In Party and declare, with some justification, that most of our problems are being caused by what the In Party is doing. The conclusion we are expected to make is that because the Out Party can perceive the connection between the In Party and the problem, they will be able to fix it if we make them the In Party. The strong supporting evidence is that before the In Party took power, when possibly the Out Party was running things, the problem was not as bad as it is today. That evidence, unfortunately, is usually to hand.

> "The two party system is like magic black and white squares which look like a staircase at one moment and a checkerboard the next."
>
> I.F. Stone, American journalist

You probably had to read that last paragraph closely to avoid being confused by the terms In Party and Out Party. It is hard to follow the thread for the reason that there is so little difference between the two. H.L. Mencken summed it up much better when he wrote in 1956: "Under democracy, one party always devotes its chief energies to trying to prove that the other party is unfit to rule - and both commonly succeed, and are right." But it is a handy mechanism for the state and helps to keep us divided in our support of one team or another.

One of the unfortunate side-effects of the new multi-party system of deciding who runs the state is that society has been fractured and turned against itself. This occurs as one group of statesmen or would-be statesmen realise they can gain power and support by blaming our problems upon a specific segment of our society, such as the rich, the poor, the whites, the blacks, the Jews, the economy, drug users, gays,

men, non-nuclear families, the non-faithful to some religion, or whatever is convenient. Their approach to dealing with whatever they perceive as a problem is always couched in the language of confrontation.
They will attack the problem, ban it, declare war on it, squeeze it till
the pips squeak, pass laws to seize its assets or force it to conform to
the norm.

They encourage some parts of our naturally changing society to view
other parts as a threat. They encourage confrontation among us because
this brings them greater power and more problems that need to be controlled. Our mind strays from the ball and we fail to recognize just what
it is that is actually retarding our ability to grow and achieve a more
ideal society. The eventual result of the divide and rule strategy is that
everybody tends to be convinced that their problems are caused by
someone else's activity. Along with this usually goes the belief that the
state can put it right if only they sort out whoever or whatever this
scapegoat is.

A classic tactic when seeking domination of a new territory, raised
to an art by the British in Empire days, was to conquer the enemy
through exploiting existing divisions or
creating new ones in a previously harmonious situation. Where existing hostile divisions existed, the alliance of
Britain with an already strong ruler
would usually guarantee the dominance of that ruler, subjugation of a

> *"Democracy is the art of
> saying 'Nice doggie' until
> you can find a rock."*
> Wynn Catlin

larger area, and almost always lead to control of that ruler by the British.

Where a harmonious situation existed, the essence was to find out
what local differences existed in races, tribes, religions, etc. and then
figure out an effective way of turning one or more of these groups
against the others. There were many techniques, such as fanning the
flames of an existing grievance, prompting an atrocity or committing
an assassination that "framed" a particular group. Of course, the aggrieved group welcomes military assistance to help them redress and
get even, and with a nip and a tuck, both sides are soon being run by a
new protective guardian who is there to protect them from each other.
Sounds familiar?

It is perhaps not difficult to see that "divide and rule" works as a handy built-in mechanism to maintain our support of the multi-party system. By convincing some of us that some others of us are a threat to their lifestyle, the state enjoins our support to protect us from each other. We easily reach a situation where each one of us thinks that some particular group or activity is responsible for most of society's and our own problems. At least the old kings and emperors only sought to protect us from others of their kind over the hill and didn't need to continually manufacture enemies within society* to maintain our fealty.

*This is not to say that it has never happened, as the Jews will attest. But since the democratic political process took root, it has become a major feature of the political arena.

"I was born on the prairies where the wind blew free and there was nothing to break the light of the sun. I was born where there were no enclosures."

Geronimo,
Apache chief (1829-1909)

14. Birthright Denied

Though we have come a long way in our evolution, we all recognise that until we developed tools and learned to manage fire, we basically lived off the land, and did so for a good while thereafter too. We still cherish stories of those who were cut off from civilisation and managed to survive in the wilderness with nothing but nature to provide. And we wring our hands with genuine concern when we hear of primitive tribes in Africa or South America being forcibly civilised or just plain wiped out by disease and avarice.

With one exception, of course, every organism on earth, plant or animal, assumes that it will live off the land with no other support structures whatsoever. The exception is us, and we are right to be proud of the major achievements we have made in creating tools and structures to advance our civilisation and remove us from the rawness of living on the edge of survival. We can keep ourselves warm in hostile climates, travel great distances with relative ease, communicate around the world with each other at low cost to our pocket or the environment, and live in houses that have evolved a long way from a makeshift tent, cave or covering of branches.

In taking these developments of our civilisation, however, and instituting them as the natural order of life, and then effectively legislating any other lifestyle out of existence, we are threatening the very ability of our civilisation to survive. Survival in this world requires evolution, change and experimentation with the established order and "way." We have always accepted that parents will look askance at their own children's lifestyle experiments and wonder what will become of the younger generation. This has been going on for years. Today's experimenters are, consciously or subconsciously, looking at ways to live that are neither dependent on the state, nor threatening and disrespectful to the earth that supports us.

> *"Do not fear to be eccentric in opinion, for every opinion now accepted was once eccentric."*
>
> Bertrand Russell (1872 - 1970)

If there is one basic right to which every human being is entitled it must be the right to LIVE OFF THE LAND on the fruits of the earth. This is the right enjoyed by every other one of God's less "civilised" creations. We have volumes of laws concerning our rights and entitlements covering areas of housing, employment, marriage, discrimination by sex, race and so forth. Yet how can this mountain of rights be of any value when the most fundamental building block of rights is not only absent but virtually a crime in most developed nations of the world - to live in a natural state on the planet earth?

It is extraordinary. Almost every other inhabitant of this planet lives off the land without even thinking about it. Yet should one of us wish to do so

> *"What men value in this world is not rights, but privileges."*
>
> *H.L. Mencken*

then we risk harassment, fines and even imprisonment. In our development of civilisation we have so surrounded ourselves with the often wonderful inventions of our species that it is quite possible to forget that the natural state of our ancestors, not that long ago, did not involve houses and apartments, motor cars, telephones, suitcases, personal documents, lawyers, stereos, policemen, television, couture and all the other trappings of life that we sometimes mistake for our life itself.

I do not suggest that the trappings of society are all evil or that we should seek to forgo them for some higher purpose. I do suggest, however, that our society is in mortal danger when it has created a climate in which to live without its trappings is considered and indeed made criminal behaviour. Such is the case in England, the United States, and most of the developed world today. In many places, including England, you are not even allowed to pursue this simple lifestyle on land in the country which you have purchased. Apparently the state and therefore the fabric of society are threatened if we should seek to live in a teepee without electricity, growing our own vegetables, rather than as a "productive" taxpaying member of society. We are NOT ALLOWED to opt out of the so-called benefits of the state, or even to choose just those that we support and believe to be good value for our taxes. Because the state has mandated our entitlement, it is deemed logical and necessary that we should HAVE TO MAKE our contribution to these benefits - as a ludicrous precondition to being alive on a given part of the planet.

This state-mandated entitlement to the benefits it offers constitutes one of the major rationales used to support the removal of our basic right as humans to move freely on our planet and to cross the red lines defining who owns which tax collection area. Of course, we must not have foreigners gaining access to the benefits we expect from the hard-earned money that our state has taken from us. That money is meant to come back to **us**, after the bureaucrats' salaries and expenses, maintenance of the military machine, foreign aid projects, European Community contributions and so forth as mentioned elsewhere herein.

The issue of land rights, or ownership of production from it, is a complex one. Many have recognized that it is impossible to personally possess and be the owner of something as indefinable as a piece of land, a section of land that is integrally looped together with the rest of the earth through feedback interchanges, sharing air and water with adjoining land. It's limits extend down into the core of the earth and upwards to some undefined level approaching a limit at, presumably, earth's atmosphere. Though no one claims to own the wind or air around us, nor the shifting waters of the seas, many now would agree we have some right and duty to keep these treasures clean.

But however we define a piece of land, we have developed entitlements and rights that we call ownership because the tenancy seems permanent. Custodianship of land and property is part of our culture and arises in many different ways, originally from the raw effort of transforming what was once raw land into a farm, a house and garden, or indeed a whole community. This process happens in nature when an oak grove makes its own environment, a city of termites changes the topography of their earth, or a pride of lions define their hunting area. Some new ideas could be developed in our society - on the nature of property rights over land, and its link to the usage and appreciation of the property. It was, after all, that usage which probably endowed it with "property-hood" in the first place. Perhaps, in the same way that we have discovered new and beneficial cures for humanity through investigating some of the medicines of "primitive" tribes, we could also gain some knowledge and possible tools from investigating their different perceptions of property rights.

Whatever rights over land and land use are indeed necessary and proper for our culture to work successfully, there can be no rationale in a sane society to deny an individual the God-given right to live off the land and to move about on it from time to time, in direct interface with our Earth. The situation becomes ridiculous when we supposedly have a "right" to a home, yet those who choose to temporarily live in a teepee, tree house or bender on so-called "common land," in a roadside lay-by, or on derelict land are forcibly evicted, fined and threatened with prison.

In the state's doomed efforts to guarantee us all decent and proper housing they have legislated out of existence any viable options between "approved" housing and a cardboard box on the streets. This is the very real void in our housing stock. Simple shelters and modest dwellings are neither difficult nor expensive to put together - they are just illegal. There are many supposedly poor countries without housing regulation in which it is unusual to find anyone sleeping permanently on the streets, let alone those who have intelligence and education.

There is no simple solution to how the state excludes from its "benefits" those who would choose not to contribute to its upkeep - those who embrace DIY culture and feel safer entrusting their health and well-being to their own efforts, rather than to the questionable abilities of the modern state. But it is patently obvious that a dangerous hypocrisy exists in a society that outwardly extols the virtues of preserving tribes in the rain forest yet allows its own citizens to be jailed for emulating such a lifestyle in their own land.

> *"Our contest is not only whether we ourselves shall be free, but whether there shall be left to mankind an asylum on earth for civil and religious liberty."*
>
> *Samuel Adams (1722-1803)*
> *American revolutionary*

"*Borders are scratched across the hearts of men*
By strangers with a calm, judicial pen,
And when the borders bleed we watch with dread
The lines of ink along the map turn red

Marya Mannes "Gaza Strip" 1959

15. The Thin Red Line

Consider for a moment that we are one of the few* creatures on this earth that may not use its own free will to move from place to place completely oblivious to red lines drawn on the map. We, the most intelligent and developed species on earth, have our movement carefully controlled and monitored by states around the world every time we seek to move across a red line on the map of our planet. It was not this way at the turn of the century and up until the First World War. Why is it that the exact location of this red line is imbued with so much significance by our society that we are willing, or expected to lay down our lives to defend it?

* Most still water fish and domestic animals are the exceptions.

One thing is certain - we will never know peace, stability or harmony in today's world as long as our lives are ruled by imaginary lines drawn by nation states upon the face of planet Earth. The world has always experienced movements of people over time, whether it was the Gauls' movement from Asia to parts of

> *"While the state exists there is no freedom, when there is freedom there will be no state."*
>
> *LENIN, The State and Revolution 1917*

Northern Europe or today's emigration of Latin Americans to sections of North America. Yet the phenomenon of the thin red line seeks to fix these boundaries permanently, once they have been naturally established.

In whose interest is it to know exactly where that line lies? If you feel a part of German culture and live in Alsace then you may well eat bratwurst and tap your feet to a brass band. If you feel French then you will act differently - that much we know. But what matters it whether someone officially decides which nation-state Alsace is a part of? It matters only to those who claim ownership over the fruits of your produce and the right to dictate your lifestyle. First and foremost the boundary defines the tax base of the government - the area from which they can take a cut of society's productivity. That this tax base may also represent some loose or coherent grouping of peoples into a similar culture base is often the case but not really relevant. That cultural base, as discussed elsewhere, was not created by government but by the people.

Ironically, the notion of nationalism is a sad manifestation of society's acceptance that somebody has got to own us, take our money from us and lay down the rules without us having much say in the matter at all. It has nothing to do with love of our country and pride in our culture. The dedicated follower of nationalism wants guys from his or her own nationality to make the rules, rather than be told what to do by foreigners. For the sake of a simple argument, let us concede that Japan makes better cars than most, China makes better fireworks, France makes better bicycles, America makes better junk food and England makes better music. So what, you ask? It might equally be argued that Switzerland makes better government; but the government isn't something you can choose - it is imposed on you by the chance of which side of a red line you were born upon. Voting, as we have discovered earlier, does not give us many options. The state would have it that nationality is something which they bestow upon us with an official document testifying to that which is already the case. If you are proud to be British then be so, but do not mix it up with the need to be officially approved by that mixed ragtag in Westminster who claim to be guardians of all things British whilst they systematically rape and destroy the society they feed upon - all those within their strongly defended red line.

Prior to the First World War and the subsequent quantum leap in size of the Western state structures, life was very different for the average citizen of these countries. With some exceptions, and not during times of war, they were generally free to travel throughout much of the world without passports, time limitations or excessive contact with bureaucracy. It was a world in which they could make home virtually anywhere, and move their money and goods from place to place with minimal interference by customs and official controls. Taxation was usually plus or minus ten percent of national income, rising above during wars and dropping back to below for most of the rest of the time.

Of course, when personal travel was less common and less restricted, it was necessary for the traveller or immigrant to support themselves wherever they chose to rest their feet. There was no question of them ever receiving support from the state running the area in which they settled - in the form of free housing, medical services, food, money and so forth. Relatives may have provided this service to an immigrant until he or she was able to become a useful member of the community and thus begin to benefit from it. Today, if you have ever travelled from country to country or around the globe you may have suspected that all the form-filling and officialdom is actually doing very little other than giving bureaucrats a raison d'etre. Hours are spent obtaining visas, queuing for customs, immigration and so forth.

In the world of the credit card, high technology and instant communications around the globe, we have the ability to positively establish identity and home-base whenever circumstances require it, using a document of some central and standard nature if convenient. This may be required by the airline taking you from A to B but not by the bus company or competing airline doing the same. It may validate your cheque or credit card, or even act as that as well. But such a document should not be a prerequisite for existence within a boundary itself, nor for travel outside of it to other parts of the culture we have established on this planet. The Internet and satellite communications are rapidly breaking down the societal barriers between our different cultural heritages. It is time also, to wither away the unnatural boundaries erected by the red tape of bureaucracy, to end the sad plight of refugees unable to leave a camp because they lack the right documents.

> "Nationalism is an infantile sickness- it is the measles of the human race."
>
> Albert Einstein (1879 - 1955)

"Find out just what any people will quietly submit to and you have the exact measure of the injustice and wrong which will be imposed upon them"

Frederick Douglas, Orator and ex-slave (1817-95)

16. Who Owns You?

You might be under the impression that your life is largely your own, to do with as you please, so long as you do not thereby immorally infringe upon other people's lives. Of course this is how we would all wish it to be and some might be so complacent as to think that it actually is that way. Yet history, today's included, continually shows us the degree to which the state regards as its own property the actual lives of the inhabitants living within the red line defining its territory. It would seem apparent that one of the unspoken rules of our world community of nations is that any individual state can do whatever it likes to its own citizens without interference from any other state.*

*If it is large enough it can also sometimes take ownership, without too much world fuss, of the people and property of a small neighbour (China/Tibet; India/Sikkhim; Indonesia/East Timor). Hitler's biggest mistake was to not quit when he was already well ahead.

This can and sometimes does extend to mass genocide - the brutal, systematic murder of millions of those within the state's own boundaries. We have seen this happen with the Armenians in Turkey early this century, a story still rarely acknowledged by anyone other than the Armenian survivors. The mass murder of German Jews and gypsies was of little concern outside Germany, until Hitler extended across his own borders and started killing foreign nationals. Pol Pot killed millions of his fellow Cambodians whilst the world looked on. Stalin murdered millions of Russian peasants and the world was not concerned. The murders continue today, whether in East Timor, the Amazon, Tiananmen Square, Waco, Nigeria - just read the Amnesty literature if you need more red spots on the world map. Even in America we find that large numbers of its own citizens are prisoners of the War on Drugs.

There is rare condemnation of these activities and even rarer action to stop them. Indeed, it is more likely that the developed and civilized nations of the world will be falling over themselves to supply the deadly tools of oppression to the states perpetrating these genocidal activities; tools such as attack helicopters and jets, weapons, electric prods, incarceration equipment and a full menu of gas from CS to old-fashioned tear gas.

One of the rare exceptions to world indifference was the peculiar case of South Africa in which ongoing world outrage was expressed at the legalized suppression of black people. This took the form of sporting boycotts and support of the blacks fighting apartheid - which probably contributed to an earlier demise of the onerous apartheid rule than would otherwise have happened. However, you can be sure that if the government of South Africa had been run by blacks subjugating blacks of another tribe there would have been no outrage and their leaders would still be having tea with the Queen and discussing their cricket scores with other world leaders today.

> *There are 16 million oppressed blacks in South Africa. But some 400 million people live elsewhere in black Africa, a majority under despotic rule. Why is so little attention given to their plight?*
>
> *George Ayittey , columnist - 1985*

Every country in the world views you as the absolute property of the state running the country of which you are a national, even though your own state will often try to persuade you that they are your servants and you are a free person. We never hear of Malaysia's draconian drug sentences when Malaysians are being executed nor of Saudi Arabians who are tortured, imprisoned or executed for their beliefs and words. But when a Filipino maid is threatened with execution in Saudi Arabia the world comes to her rescue.

An individual state might take strong military action when its own borders or its citizens are threatened by another state. But it has always historically and continues today to stop short of ever taking effective action against another state that chooses to massacre or persecute its own citizens.* The concept of one state interfering in another's affairs is not really even considered, though occasionally some United Nations rescue mission may appear too late on the scene and contrive to make the existing situation even more entrenched. A classic case of this was the 'UNsafe' zones set up in the former Yugoslavia. The holocaust continues with a new cast of victims each year.

---

*That does not preclude it from abusing those citizens, however, when seeking to settle a score with their leader. Indeed, after the Gulf War, America's chosen means to persecute its enemy Sadaam Hussein was to wreak poverty and disease upon the citizens of his country through browbeating their trade partners into an international boycott. It is unlikely, however that Sadaam Hussein's own food or medical supplies were ever interrupted.

Of course, the political structure depends very much upon this perception of ownership, since each government exists solely because it has the ability to dictate to the people within its boundaries how they live and behave, and to regularly and "officially" take as much of their money from them as it deems possible. That this has to be done within some framework of law matters little when we see the speed with which basic laws safeguarding our freedom or setting our taxation, are changed in order to pursue one political agenda after another.

The top-gun, self-serving power structure
Also claims outright ownership
Of the lives of all those born
Within their sovereignly claimed
Geographical bounds
And can forget their citizens' lives
In their official warfaring
Which, of psychological necessity
Is always waged in terms
Of moral rectitude
While covertly protecting and fostering
Their special self-interests.

Buckminster Fuller - ETHICS - A Geoview

IN Bolivia, a clown known only as "Mr Twister" has been threatened with prison for refusing to promise a Santa Cruz court that he would not repeat his offence. Mr Twister was charged with repeatedly feeding the parking meters of complete strangers.

Report in the Guardian, June 96

17. Victimless Crimes

A vast amount of effort and resources is expended trying to prevent members of the public from doing things that can harm no one but themselves, and probably do not even do that. In most cases the prohibition is against doing something that may carry a slight risk of harm. In fact, tens of thousands of lives are actually damaged, just in order to stop people from willingly exposing themselves to possible danger or damage through drug use, dangerous sports, unusual sex, illegal parties, alternative medicines, or other forms of activity not sanctioned by the state. The state has various ways to protect us from exposing ourselves to things that they think could somehow harm us. They can take our money away in fines, confiscate our property, put us in jail, get us fired or liquidate our business. Hell...there are even situations where they can kill you to protect you from yourself. Even the right to take your own life is an offence in most parts of the world.* We can see from this alone that the state views our very lives as somehow belonging to it and not to us.

*I have this mad picture in my mind of a crouching policeman, shouting: "Don't jump or I'll shoot!" to some would-be suicide at the edge of the cliff top.

The state, in the interests of governing the nation, has no right whatsoever to pass laws supposedly protecting us from ourselves. Their basic remit for existence is to protect us from others who would seek to attack us, or steal the property we have fairly earned through our own endeavours. In fact, the state that should protect us now makes the largest attack on our property of all - the institutionalized theft of approximately half of the value we add to creation every year (see Money's Real Dimension). Much of this stolen wealth is then turned against us - literally used to attack us when we choose to explore or do or witness or create things that are a threat to no one but perhaps ourselves.

Numerous scientific studies over several decades have shown cannabis use itself to be harmless. In centuries of usage, there has not been a death laid at the door of this innocuous drug. Yet thousands are arrested and processed at great expense through courts and prisons for indulging in this happier and safer alternative to alcohol. The rapid growth in prison building in both America and Britain is fuelled by drug cases - an attack by the state on its own citizens. Some 60% of the prisoners in U.S. Federal jails are there for drug offences, which are usually non-violent. At the moment one-fourth of all the young black men in America are either in prison or on parole. Jailing and confiscating the property of citizens who like to puff cannabis or take other drugs neither benefits their lives nor serves any need of society.

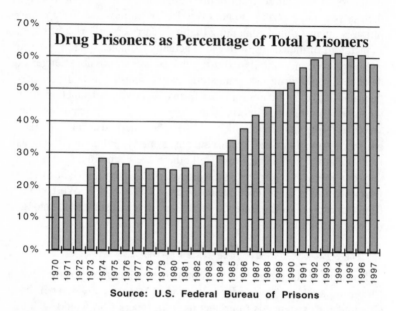

Drug Prisoners as Percentage of Total Prisoners

Source: U.S. Federal Bureau of Prisons

People have been imprisoned, harassed and had their children taken into state care as a result of rejecting the official educational system approved by the state. Presumably the future of their children, as productive members of society, might be jeopardized if the state did not legislate just what they should all learn. Why should the state treat this as such a threat? It could be argued that the official educational system, with its centrally standardized curricula, does not always set a hard example to beat. Educational standards in countries such as England and the United States are regularly trounced by so-called third world countries. Our own culture is filled with stories of peasants and uneducated immigrants who ended up magnates and still manage to do so today. The founder of the worldwide Holiday Inn hotel chain, who left school when he was thirteen, was fond of quipping: "When you ain't got no education you gotta fall back on your brains." His special skill was knowing where to place a new hotel - not something that had been covered in his schooling.

The state has come to see itself as more responsible for your child than you. And if they decide you are not being a good enough parent then they, the ultimate parent, will step in and take over, forcibly removing children from "unfit" parents. Though we read daily of the abuse and assaults upon children in state-run homes and of their magnetic attraction for paedophiles, these state supported abusers of children are rarely raided by the social services. The cases only seem to come to light after many years of bureaucratic obstructions and cover-ups; then broad inquiries are held, often without any prosecution of the perpetrators.

Sex, our primary means of producing children, is another arena in which the state thinks it necessary to protect us from danger. Whether in print, film, the market, or the bedrooms of consenting adults, sex is regulated the world over by laws deemed to be for our own good. Many authors have been jailed and censured for writing about the joys of the basic mechanism maintaining the survival of our species. A similar fate has met publishers, film-makers and performers seeking to include sex in their subject matter. Conversely, those human acts that damage our species can be freely written about, or portrayed in print or films graphically depicting murder, injury and destruction. What is so wrong with sex, that the depiction of it in print or film must be so controlled by law? It is curious that "sex and violence" are so often joined together when people are in a condemning mood. - considering the opposite ends of the spectrum at which they exist.

Across the world, there still exist vast volumes of law and regulation dictating what consenting adults may do, for pleasure, within the privacy of their own homes. Some of these consenting adults may have sex with those of the same gender, use orifices that are prohibited by law from being pleasure receptacles or even include painful and strange activity. Some of the stranger sexual practices may have been caused by the repression of more "natural" tendencies earlier in life. Must we really have a government legislating what is acceptable for people to do with their own bodies, for their own pleasure? If society or a local culture chooses to shun or reject people because of their chosen lifestyle or sexual tendencies then it will. But we should not endure a situation in which the state is empowered to harass and imprison such people - or indeed legislate their mandatory acceptance. The natural evolution of society should be relied upon to eventually accept, or adapt, that which is created from within its own dynamic.

We have nothing to fear from those who seek to live their own lives

outside whatever the currently legislated norms of society are. If someone's choice is to live in a home-made tent in the woods without the
benefit (and ecological cost) of hot and cold running water, central
heating and flushing toilet, then who are we or the state, to say that this
constitutes an illegal dwelling and to treat them like criminals? The
faulty thinking process that guides the state when regulating the status
quo goes something like this: "But imagine what would happen if everybody did this - it would be total chaos."* They fail to realize that
most people like toilets and television, plumbing, power and many of
the other conveniences of life. Everybody is not going to run out and
live in a tree or a tent on common ground if they stop arresting and
harassing anyone who does. But those who did so of choice would certainly reduce their need for state assistance, housing stock, and ever
more infrastructure.

*The actual words uttered to this author in 1991, when a beautifully painted fractal
pavement appeared in front of my Strange Attractions shop devoted to chaos
theory. The council team were there within two days to dig it all up and put new
grey paving down. I queried the *why* of it with the local bureaucrat in charge, and
this is what he said verbatim, whilst complimenting us on the work. Meanwhile
two burnt out abandoned cars littered the same road for two months, endanger-
ing children and looking pretty ugly. I contemplated starting a "terrorist" group
after this which would have gone out in the dead of night to paint pretty pictures
around dangerous potholes that needed filling.

There are countless examples of the state's obsession with our private lives and businesses and how we live them and run them. At the
core of it all is the assumption that the state knows best: that given the
resources (your resources), they are better able to direct your life than
you are. Of course, since all the state knows is the status quo, the bulk
of its regulation will be directed at maintaining their view of what the
current culture constitutes. Many of those whom society now views as
cultural heroes - the great performers, thinkers, and inventors of history
- were, in their day, imprisoned, ridiculed and harassed.

In addition to all the laws that supposedly protect us from ourselves
or others, we have a growing mountain of laws designed to mandate
our compliance with government demands. There is no real victim involved in these crimes, and they have grown most of all in the U.S.A.
The forfeiture laws of America, and now the UK, were initially brought
in to fight "the drug menace" and are increasingly being extended to
many other areas deemed criminal. The first extension was into banking where all cash transactions above a thousand dollars or so are
classed as suspicious, with clerks and employees earning rewards by
reporting such transactions. The owner of the money then has it for-

feited until and unless they can produce the records proving that it arose from a legitimate, tax-paid transaction. An immigrant community leader, returning to her native country with some $10,000 of locally collected charitable contributions had it seized and suffered a further fine for non-completion of a simple reporting form. Forfeiture law was most recently applied to individually practicing doctors in the U.S., accelerating the move by doctors from private practice to health companies. It is now deemed a criminal offence to make any clerical error in a patient's records, such as a wrong date or diagnosis code. Though the law was ostensibly brought in to help prevent fraud against insurance companies, there is no need for the error to have any fraudulent or medical consequences. During the law's first year of operation, in 1997, over $1 Billion in assets was taken by the government from doctors who had neither had a trial nor been proved to have done anything wrong.

The demands for compliance with tax laws are based upon the flimsy premise that by not paying the state it's demands, you are somehow stealing from the other good citizens who do pay their fealty. But the state must be fed so we can understand why this class of crime is so covered in law. But in America today, simple businessmen increasingly face jail and heavy fines for failing for return forms that are solely intended for statistical purposes. Bizarre as it might seem to anyone who has not yet read this far, much of today's new legislation in "the land of the free" seems to be geared towards finding more ways to steal people's money from them and put them in jail.

As we have seen, an increasing amount of today's law is not concerned with our protection at all, but with our conformity to government regulations and permitted behaviour. I suggest that the ratio between these two types of laws could be used as an indicator of the degree to which any given state has tipped towards being termed "totalitarian."

This shift in attitudes towards the function of state policing of society is reflected in the changed terminology for police in the U.S.A. They no longer refer to themselves as "peace officers" since this is a misnomer. They more accurately call themselves "law-enforcement officers," which makes more sense when we consider that much of their activity involves the forceful and often violent interruption of otherwise quite peaceful activity.

The whole concept of the victimless crime is at the heart of the breakdown of "law and order" so lamented by both citizens and politicians. Vast sums are spent, and armies of bureaucrats and police maintained, to ensure that we comply with needless regulations, primarily designed to keep things as the government would like them - regulations which block the natural evolution of our species. Of course these resources should be spent to stop real crime and its causes, but as long as the state is running things **it will be in the long term interest of the prison service to have more prisons and of the police to have more crime.**

INCARCERATION RATES around the world

Country	Inmates per 100,000 population
Russia	690 **
United States	519 *
Ukraine	390 **
South Africa	368 *
Singapore	229 *
Romania	200 **
Hong Kong	179 *
England	93 *
France	84 *
Germany	80 *
Turkey	80 **
Ireland	55 **
Japan	36 *
Cambodia	26 **
Phillipines	26 **
India	24 * and**

*   Associated Press, Sept 12, 1994.
** 1995, Americans Behind Bars: U.S. and International Use of Incarceration

After viewing the above figures, it becomes more apparent why the U.S.A. often paints itself in the image of the global policeman. Most aid money and commercial permits require that recipients and trade partners enforce various laws designed to spread a global morality moulded on "the American way." It reminds us of the arrogance of Christian missionaries putting clothes on natives lest they be corrupted by their nakedness. From the numbers above, it would seem there is good potential for the export of prison technology to all those countries less diligent at enforcing their laws. There must be a few million chillum-smoking sadhus breaking cannabis laws in India alone. The U.S.A. and UK now take pride in training police and paramilitary all over the world in the newest techniques of civilian surveillance and crowd control.

A Nepalese vendor of used flashlight parts

18. Poverty and Crime - a popular myth

It has almost become an accepted truth in the Western world today that poverty is one of the fundamental causes of crimes against property, crimes that have victims. That this is both untrue and baseless becomes obvious with but a moment's reflection on the situation. Crime stems not from a lack of wealth but from a lack of morality, and I will argue that a lack of morality is not the exclusive preserve of, nor even a natural consequence of being "poor." It is an insult to the financially lacking, who constitute a majority of the world's population, to suggest that immorality is a natural consequence of their lack of monetary wealth. Many of these communities indeed show a far lower level of crime than we experience in the West, and manage to lead richer lives than many a neurosis-ridden city dweller.

Today you can travel to countless countries around the globe which have massive differentials between the rich and the poor and yet suffer relatively low levels of crime compared to the affluent Western cities such as London, Amsterdam, Miami or Toronto. Take Bombay for instance, where the poor live in what many would consider dismal conditions, sometimes sleeping on the street or in the most makeshift of hovels; living by begging or bare sustenance activity. Within this milieu the wealthy of Bombay are very rich with housing prices reputedly the highest in the world. Yet you can leave your bicycle unlocked anywhere in Bombay with minimal fear of theft, and you can walk through this diverse city at day or night feeling safer than you would in the urban jungles of most developed countries. This is the case not only in Bombay, but in numerous third world cities around the world,* whose poor would find it difficult to comprehend the standards used to define those that we deem to be below the "poverty line". We are indeed poverty stricken in the West, but not in the financial department.

*Poverty and crime are undoubtedly found in combination sometimes; though it is unlikely that the street thieves of Rio de Janeiro are any more lacking in morality, or damaging to our planet, than those who happily take Brazilian government grants to cut down the rainforest.

In the Western world, we have suffered great periods of financial poverty such as that of the Great Depression of 1930, when many people lived on their wits with no social net to protect them. Though many lost everything they had owned and soup lines formed in the streets, levels of crime and murder did not soar to anything like today's record levels. Petty crimes of the unauthorised food consumption variety may have been higher but a huge section of society did not lose their basic morality when they lost their money.

Bonnie and Clyde achieved fame because of their uniqueness - this kind of stuff did not go on every day, and they certainly did not make a lot of money, even adjusting for inflation. Though extremes of poverty and wealth existed in the so-called Wild West of 19th century America, the chance of being murdered or mugged or burgled was remote compared to that which exists in these same places today. Bank and train robberies and shoot-outs were rare events remembered for years after. That gunfight at the OK Corral just happened once and it went into legend. Jesse James was a one-off.

We are prone to trivialise our own value and wealth by insisting on such a linear scorecard. We end up totalling all the stuff that was sold for money in a particular geographical area, and dividing it by the number of humans *being* there, when last counted, arriving thereby at the average "per capita" wealth of that country. I ask you! What about the wealthiness of good health, happiness, an unpolluted environment, fullness of love, friends and family, and a freedom from rules and regulation by Big Brother?

I will argue that a rural Thailand peasant in a happy self-sufficient community, eating pure food and breathing pure air, free of debt, far removed from sources of pollution both environmental and mental, largely removed from bureaucracy, taxation, and regulation, is IN FACT A WEALTHIER PERSON than a deeply neurotic sales executive in New York, unsure of his job security in a soul-destroying industry who financially earns perhaps 100 times as much as our Thai peasant, but still not enough to meet his mortgage and loan repayments plus living expenses and child support. Maybe we need a few more words for different forms of poverty.

Unnecessary laws, prohibitions, and regulations which are rigidly maintained by law-enforcement officers are patently one of the single greatest sources of crime in this world; and, as you will understand from the rest of this book, they are also one of the great contributing factors towards poverty of all forms. Worst of all, they discourage us as a society from developing our own codes of morality and make it easier for criminals to view their crimes as thwarting the state and breaking its stupid rules, rather than as committing an offence against the society to which the criminal belongs. The distinction is becoming dangerously blurred between what is a true crime against a fellow human, and what is just a transgression of some law that seeks to standardize behaviour rather than protect a potential victim.

"I used to think I was poor. Then they told me I was not poor, I was needy. They told me it was self-defeating to think of myself as needy, I was deprived. Then they told me underprivileged was overused. I was disadvantaged. I still do not have a dime but I have a great vocabulary."

Jules Feiffer, American humorist

*"The press is
the living jury
of the nation"*
James Gordon Bennett
newspaper editor - c.1830

*"The danger hat the press may misunder-
stand or misinterpret or even misinform is in
the final analysis a small price to pay compared to the services the news media render
when they expose wrongdoing or gross errors
of judgement by the powers that be."*
Leonard H. Marks, lawyer 1995

19. So What's News?

History is a continuing catalogue of how those who think they run the planet waste vast sums of money attempting to maintain the status quo or to alter it against another nation's will by force. This takes the form of wars of attrition and defence, subsidy, controls, and endless strictures as to what is and is not a house, a car, an eating apple, a legal party and endless other matters. The daily news is dominated either by plans, programmes, and proposals by politicians; or by the failure, collapse, wars and scandals that are now the result of the plans, programmes, and proposals about which we were reading in the years gone by. Next time you look at a newspaper take note of how much of it is dominated by the above. Only the names and the places change from week to week.

The so-called news is dominated by activities of the politicians and the state, yet it would seem anything that is truly new and lasting in society comes from the people and not the politicians. In fact the world's politicians seem to do the same old thing over and over again - which is to tell us what to do and beat us over the head if we don't listen. When they start telling each other what to do it often leads to a fight in which we, as innocent bystanders, also get beaten over the head (i.e. bombed, shelled, jailed, shot).

Yet despite its tendency to fill our heads with all the above, the media also performs a valuable service for society. It can often be seen to do a better job at monitoring and exposing the abuses and iniquities of our world than does the state. As we know, the state is usually the last to acknowledge its own corruption and abuse, and then only after revelation in the media. The media is often the first to inform us of scandals involving large or small corporations and dangers facing us through exposure to environmental chemicals or diseases in the food chain. Were we relying solely on government bulletins, we would know little of oil spills in the oceans, corruption in government, rising asthma among children, Mad Cow Disease, radiation leaks and linked diseases, Gulf War syndrome, the disappearing ozone hole or endangered species. Regular radio and TV programmes are dedicated to airing consumer grievances against companies, providing negative advertising for the business concerned, and cautioning us all against using that company or its faulty products. This is a service which society needs and by providing it the media attracts our attention. We could, perhaps use a few more fearless investigative reporters (and editors). Fortunately, the new technology of publishing, together with the world-wide net of global communication is dramatically expanding the scope of the media, and access to it.

20. The State of Business

Much of the structure of today's so-called "free economy" is distorted by the state's involvement. At the top of this distortion is that dictated by the state's need to extract taxation efficiently and regularly from anyone engaged in any sort of activity involving a medium of exchange. The core need of the state is to raise as much money every year as possible - regardless of how, where or from whom it is taken and how, where and on what it is spent. This short-term attitude pervades modern business ethics because of the penalty the tax man applies for taking a long term view of how you wish to manage the assets of your own or your shareholders' business. When profit is not spent quickly on new equipment, expansion or other growth of the business, a painfully large chunk of it seems somehow to end up with the taxman.

In the days of not that long ago (a hundred years) companies all over the world used to keep most of their profits, sometimes piles of profits. Even after paying for the big houses, jewellery and servants there was a lot left over. With it they made long-term investments in the original infrastructure of canals, railways, communication, underground transport systems, housing, power supply, bridges, and more. They spent their own money and if the project screwed up, it cost them. They also set up quite a few universities and social institutions. Today, most big projects in the private sector involve significant levels of bank financing, with the inherent priority being structured and rapid repayment, rather than long-term investment.

The real cost to our species of this short term thinking, engendered for the sake of the tax man's convenience, is possibly greater than the worth of the money that is raised each year. Many other areas of business are structured, not in the interests of the business or its customers, but because of government regulation.

LIMITED LIABILITY is a distortion of natural business which the state somehow thinks is a benefit to society. The concept did not exist at the beginning of the 19th century and came into legislation during the middle of it. Simply put, limited liability (indicated by "Ltd." or "plc" after the company name) makes it legal to break commitments and walk away from the mess you created. This is possible because, by government permission, you are allowed to be a "limited company" instead of a person or a group of people interacting with the rest of the world. Since time immemorial, governments have walked away from their messes and they figure it is all right for businesses to do so too, provided that they pay their taxes and play by the rules that the state has set. Society never developed any such mechanism on its own; notwithstanding occasional extenuating circumstances, we work as a society by honouring and being responsible for our debts and commitments.

Thus you might agree that, if I convince you my brand of shampoo is best for your hair, which in fact makes it all fall out, then I have a liability to do more than just give you back the money I took. However, with limited liability, I can be so incompetent that I accidentally sell thousands of bottles of this corrosive shampoo and end up with thousands of customers who want their money back plus an expensive wig. Well, that is just too much for the pockets of my Limited Liability Company, so I call in the liquidator, drive to my country house in the Rolls Royce, sit by the swimming pool and decide what to do next. You don't even get your money back. Of course, when this sort of abuse occurs we will need to have the government legislate precise new standards for hair shampoo to safeguard our scalps in the future. Luckily for us, most people making hair shampoo recognise that happily hirsute customers make them more money in the long term.

Ironically, the state further compounds the immoral protection of limited liability not just by making it available but by posing the greatest threat from which the individuals operating any company would wish to be protected. The vast majority of companies forced into receivership are pushed there because of unpaid taxes, often ones which they are commanded to collect on behalf of the government. And those taxes are collected from whatever is left of the company's assets

> ### NEWS REPORT
>
> **Mr Bertram describes the case of an Edinburgh fish-and-chip shop forced into insolvency by the vigorous attentions Customs. The collector decided the owner had suppressed sales and under-declared VAT returns by £20,600. To contest that figure, the owner had to post that amount with the tribunal court beforehand. He was unable to find the money, the business collapsed, and Customs received nothing.**

before the remainder is allocated to banks, creditors, and unfulfilled customers.

TAXATION itself has other side effects apart from siphoning off wealth and encouraging short-term thinking. Many large companies and wealthy individuals expend considerable resources and set up complicated protection schemes, which lock up money in offshore havens that might otherwise have been reinvested in the local environment. This is an artificially stimulated loss to the community. Moreover, all that top brainpower devoted to this effort is a waste of human intellect, which should have nothing to do with the goals and objectives of any human enterprise, collective or otherwise.

Because we take it for granted, it is difficult to conceive the size of the impact that taxation has on the basic running of a business. Tax can often be the single greatest cost passed onto the consumer purchasing products or services. The tax accumulates with import duties, excise taxes, employee taxes, business rates, Value Added Tax, benefits-in-kind tax, and a whole host of money-grabbing mechanisms around the world. Then, if that business manages to take in more money than it spends (makes a profit), a further chunk is taken in corporation tax. That businesses spend a lot of time considering the tax-implications of their activities and means of reducing the overall impact on product cost is understandable. Even without this intent, the basic accounting for and tracking of taxes is a major brain drain on the management of any enterprise. The unfortunate effect of this is a diversion from the actual remit of a business, which is to serve its customers, and a substantial added on cost to almost every product we consume.

The state depends upon big business to implement its relentless TAXATION OF THE INDIVIDUAL, something that has been instinctively resisted by many generations of individuals before us. If you were relying upon other people's earnings to support yourself, wouldn't you prefer to tax 20,000 people's income through a single employer, rather than have to deal with that many hairdressers, market traders, greengrocers, builders, gardeners and wandering musicians? I think so, and it is no accident, nor in the interests of the general public, that government policy over the past twenty years has encouraged the growth of large corporate culture. Simultaneously, business rates, parking restrictions, developments and many other measures make today's retailing environ-

> *"The art of taxation consists in so plucking the goose to obtain the largest amount of feathers, with the least possible amount of hissing."*
>
> Jean-Baptiste Colbert,
> treasurer to Louis XIV.

ment increasingly hostile to anyone other than the chain stores. The vast reams of regulations, and the requirements of accounting for taxation, place such burdens upon anyone seeking to "do business" as an individual that effectively, most are weeded out. Many people could run a small venture by the "seat of their pants," if freed from the need to understand double-entry bookkeeping, VAT accounting, P.A.Y.E. and the intricacies of employer/employee regulations. It should not be made so difficult to find a way of fitting into our society and providing a useful service or product to others.

Another major distortion of the natural evolution of business in society is created by giant GOVERNMENT SCHEMES designed to protect and promote certain industries - even when they are outdated and delivering overpriced product. Nuclear power could never have developed in a state-free world - it does not make any economic sense and is uninsurable. Not even the most notorious industrialist of the 19th century would have jeopardized his entire wealth on such an uninsurable risk. Who could cover the possible loss of the entire UK, an area the size of that made toxic by Chernobyl? Well, **we do** because our state thinks nuclear power is a good thing and that, if the entire country has to be evacuated, we'll somehow all muck together to foot the bill; with what, the handouts at the refugee camps?

Billions are still squandered by the Common Agricultural Policy because the thought of dismantling it is too shocking for the bu-

> Independent on Sunday - May 1995
>
> Just 20 years ago the International Atomic Energy Agency confidently predicted that there would be 4,450 thousand megawatts of nuclear capacity worldwide by the year 2000; now the industry will be lucky to achieve 360 thousand megawatts by the same time, just 8 per cent of this target.
>
> What went wrong? The seeds of failure were sown right back at that moment of hope and hype, the opening of Calder Hall.

reaucrats who make a living perpetuating its depredations. Environmentally damaging and economically questionable dam projects are pursued in developing nations, because the money has been donated by Western states eager to secure lucrative contracts for their friends in business. Roads are often built for the sake of budget fulfilment, using the handy state mechanism of compulsory purchase to overcome any natural opposition by homeowners refusing to sell what they rightfully own. Objectors are arrested or hauled out by bailiffs. England's Department of Trade and Industry's budget in 1993/1994 was

£3,600,000,000 to be spent helping British industry be more competitive at home and abroad. Imagine how much more competitive these businesses would have been had that £ 3.6 billion not been removed from their earnings, and their customer's pockets in the first place.

We frequently hear businesses bemoaning the costs of unnecessary government REGULATION. They are often justified since much government regulation of business is out of date or inappropriate to the situation. It is confrontational and not co-operative. Very few businesses would actually survive if they did comply with all the regulation directed at them. Despite all the regulations, when negligent errors are made the state imposed consequences are usually inappropriate and focused more on fines than compensation for the victims. A very simple example of this regulation gone mad will be familiar to anyone who has ever operated a business involving plant and equipment. When you consider the safety regulations associated with this equipment, you will rapidly appreciate that the hazardous activity of sticking a four-pointed object in and out of our mouth dozens of times every day breaks every rule in the book. Will the day ever come when all forks require cheek guards and eye protectors?

Safety standards, codes of practice and responsibility need to be an integral part of the natural government of the business world, and in today's climate this is sometimes lacking in businesses, whether at multi-national level or that of a market stall. But most of the time it is there and this is apparent every time you buy a product that does not make you want to write a complaint letter to the manufacturers.

We do already rely on standards and regulations which are effective and flexible and so invisible that we can easily fail to appreciate them. On a simple level, it was Heinz who set the original standard for baked beans and Bic who did so for disposable cigarette lighters. Not an awful lot has changed since they did so - without state interference. Many trades form societies to set standards for registered members so that the consumer can avoid uninsured architects or untrained acupuncturists. State protection is a poor substitute for consumer awareness though it would be comforting to think that you didn't have to concern yourself with too much detailed monitoring when out roaming in the market. The commercial potential for a relevant service, or services, to maintain standards and monitor consumer products is raised in a later chapter.

The state often gives FALSE LEGITIMACY to businesses who would otherwise have no means to exist nor place in existence. As mentioned earlier, this is patently the case with nuclear power, which dangerous and uneconomic activity would never have merited any chance of existence in a free economy. Unless exonerated by the state, companies do have responsibility in common law for their activities. The nuclear power companies could never accept responsibility for their outdated plant* nor will any free insurance company insure for the risk of accident.

*The working life of a nuclear power plant is from 30-60 years. Its toxic lifetime lasts a further several thousand years, and some elements, such as spent fuel rods, can remain dangerous for 20,000 years.

The principle and practice of artificial fertilization of the soil with nitrogen and phosphates metaphorically exploded with Uncle Sam's efforts after World War II to find another use for the outputs of its giant munitions industry. It is the similarity between explosives and fertilizers that makes it so easy for terrorists to convert the one to the other. It now seems clear that the subsequent artificial boosting of crop yield with chemical fertilizers led to weaker food crops with less resistance to insects, fungi, and weeds. This weakened food crop now requires regular dosing with an ever-stronger arsenal of chemicals poisons to keep the competition at bay. We are fighting a war against the land that feeds us, undermining the natural mechanisms with which it works its magic in our mechanistic attempt, not to feed the world, but to feed the world cheap meat, and supply cheap ingredients to the food processing industry. The enormous hidden costs of state-supported cheap food policy are gradually becoming apparent.

The vast bulk of the arms industry has but one end customer - the state or would-be state. Many poorly considered international projects with neither merit nor chance of profit are proceeded with at enormous cost, having arisen through the conditions attached to aid money by the donor state. These, and many other enterprises that waste rather than return our effort, or return a very short economic benefit at great long-term cost, are unnecessarily in existence due to the state's giving them a false legitimacy.

Finally,* the state's pervasive regulation and control of business has the effect of stifling the enterprise of our species. It makes it increasingly difficult for an individual with a bright idea to go into business, or even someone with any old idea for that matter. An early insight into this restrictive climate came some years ago at a cafe in Marrakesh, where I noticed a young man on the corner each evening with a packet of 20 cigarettes, selling them singly to passers-by. The customers were able to better manage their "habit" by buying the cigarettes singly. And the young man was able to set up his own business as a retailer for the cost of a packet of cigarettes. This is an almost inconceivable concept in our developed democracies. The bridge is great between what is required to manage our own enterprise, and what is required to do so to the requirements of the state. Many are unable to cross this bridge, despite having all the skills that nature demands to interact in this way with the society around them.

*This "finally" is for the purposes of this chapter. There are countless other general and specific ways in which the state distorts the nature of free enterprise between individuals and companies. In Great Britain, the state's legislation has led to some 85% of the UK's listed companies now being owned by giant pension funds; what a state to be in...

Companies and those engaged in business do need to take responsibility for their activities and for the wider costs of their operations and we, as a society including those businesses, need to evolve means for this to happen. I suggest that without the grotesque and massive interference by the state in the regular day-to-day transactions of mankind (which we call enterprise or business), the mechanisms to provide this wider responsibility would have evolved in the natural course of events. We are not going to make business more responsible by giving up this responsibility to the state.

Indeed, one of the disturbing developments of modern times is the ongoing attempt by large multi-nationals corporations to manipulate and actually govern the mechanism of the state. Of course, this could be seen as the first stirring of the latest change in the long chain of command - as mentioned earlier (pharaoh, emperor, senate, church, king, president, parliament ... multi-national). Why not? Because coercion does not work as a stable means to govern our society, and thereby our society's evolution. Multi-national corporations are no more able to effectively dictate evolution than are democratically elected parliaments or the church.

Guardian - March 1998

ONE of Britain's biggest supermarket chains took on the might of US agriculture yesterday by refusing to use genetically modified plants and bacteria in its own-brand food products.

Iceland guarantees that from May 1 nearly 400 grocery lines will not contain rogue genes, technically known as mutant lifeforms, which are designed to make products last longer or taste better.

Positive News - March 1998

Swissair has become the first airline to serve organic food.

Initially, the new Healthy Fare over the Clouds', is being introduced on flights leaving Switzerland as the supplies are not available to provide 'Natural Gourmet' meals on flights leaving other countries.

But Swissair Chief Executive, Philip Bruggisser, says, "By the year 2000 we want to ensure that 90% of the products we use to prepare our meals our organically grown." It will take the

21. Global Corporation Inc.

We worry about the nightmare scenario of a world run by big business, controlling our minds with advertising, filling our lives with material junk and devastating our earth in their eternal quest for a quick buck. The most frightening manifestation of this is the faceless multinational, plying its trade with tentacles in every country of the world. Some of these companies will sell products with known health risks in markets where they are still legally declared safe. We have heard of the healthy mothers in Africa encouraged to formula feed their babies. Large cola companies have bought up the local competition and pumped their own product into the market. This all happens, and in the absence of some central Commissar of Production will continue to happen. It does occur less often, however, when markets become educated.

As mentioned in the last chapter, many aspects of business have been shaped by state intervention; we also have many examples of big business intervening in the affairs of the state, prompting this or that regulation, subsidy or permission and even sometimes extending to a landgrab and subsequent murder of the previous custodians. This chapter is not meant to be an apology for the moral transgressions of many businesses but it is intended to make you aware of the fundamental difference between the relationship we develop with business and the relationship we have with the State.

So you might as well get to know your local multinational because they are going to be an increasingly important part of the future. To help you recover from the shock, let me point out a few things about businesses, small and large.

POINTS

Many multinationals now have sales greater than the GNP of most of the world's nation states. Despite the power this gives them, as they get even larger they will be less and less likely to ever find a reason to rain bombs upon us, their global customers. This is so unlikely for any business that very few, if any, of today's multinationals have a special reserve of bombs stored away - just in case the need arises. This cannot be said of today's nation states.

Not many businesses will put you in jail, fine you or harass you if you just don't want to buy their product; however brilliantly clever the advertising you don't respond to, however many millions they spend promoting it, or however much they know you need it. There is a choice and even though a lot of people are "fighting it out" in the marketplace, rarely does anyone actually get maimed or killed and, with footwear for instance, we end up with a choice of shoes, sandals, slippers, sneakers, thongs, skis, roller blades and boots. We have leather boots, rubber boots, canvas boots, space boots, wading boots; in all colours, sizes, and styles.

It is not unusual for business to respond pretty quickly to consumer needs and demands. Even if big companies are sometimes slow to respond, they spend many millions trying to determine just what it is the consumer wants. When small flexible companies do this they often grow faster, steal an edge on the competition, and make more money...thus getting bigger.

Companies usually stop short of killing or imprisoning their competition and critics. Even that early multinational, IBM, effectively controlling the world computing market in the early 1970's, could only stand by and watch whilst two young nerds in a California garage* changed the world of computers with the introduction of the Apple computer. Many big businesses got to be where they are by starting out small with a brilliant new product that made all of our lives a lot easier or more enjoyable in some way. Other small companies got big by responding to consumers faster than the established giants of their industry. Companies can and do sue for damages if defamed by critics, but as the "McLibel" case against McDonalds has dramatically shown, such tactics can backfire when the criticisms are defensible.** The McDonalds case turned into one of the greatest "own goals" of corporate history. Since "winning," millions more of a harder-hitting "What's Wrong With McDonalds" leaflet have been and continue to be distributed, and the McSpotlight internet site, arising from the case, became one of the most popular sites in cyberspace.

** I refer to Steve Woszniac and Stephen Jobs who created Apple Computers and the Macintosh. With minimal resources they successfully challenged and changed the most firmly emplaced corporate monopoly of history. The chairman of IBM had predicted in 1949 that the world market would eventually reduce to five giant computers - Apple changed all that.

*Helen and Dave, two unemployed Britons with the bulldog spirit intact, defended themselves against libel charges by McDonalds rather than say they were sorry, and went into the record books with the longest libel case, and then the longest court case in UK history. The award-winning website devoted to the issue can be found at - www.mcspotlight.org

Few companies claim the right or even harbour the desire, to break into your house at any time of day and night to ensure that you are not ingesting, reading or watching something of which they disapprove. This even applies if you choose to watch some devastatingly revealing, dirt-digging video produced by a new start-up company, whose stated aim is to put the brand-leader right out of business. Even if you have been drinking Pepsi every day of your life for years, you can switch overnight to water, orange juice or beer without so much as a veiled threat from the Pepsi company.

> *"A business must have a conscience as well as a counting house."*
>
> Sir Montague Burton, the tailor

Many companies offer a guarantee with their product, so that if the promised washing machine never arrives or breaks down completely, you have an opportunity to correct the situation. The commercial principle and practice of offering guarantees existed long before legislation made it mandatory. You usually do get what you are promised and if there are, say, only four cans of beer in the six-pack, then you can actually point this out to the vendor and get some money refunded. The growing weight of overall taxation on business and its employees may well have reduced the level of back-up service that the average consumer might expect to accompany their product purchase. I remember when my mother spilt some Copydex glue on our carpet in the 1950's. She wrote to the company asking for advice on how to remove it. Within twenty four hours their local representative was at our doorstep with a bottle of the appropriate solvent and help with its application; of course, she has used Copydex ever since.

Businesses do quite commonly sack disgraced and dishonest executives. We occasionally read of this in the newspapers and rarely find that the executives move on to greater and higher positions in the firms or are retired early for medical reasons with full pay. When internal corruption is discovered it is quite common for those involved to be dismissed with no consideration at all. Sometimes corporate bigshots may get an undeserved "golden handshake" if there are no legal grounds for their removal, but life will always have some warts.

Holding onto a monopoly in a free world is not as easy as you might think. Whilst the government maintains the (one and only) Monopolies Commission to check abuses, there are few examples of a long and stable <u>corporate</u> monopoly in history that did not rely upon state support and legislation. Few unsupported monopolies survive long against competition and changes in our culture. Most of the long-term monopolies we seem to have experienced are those regulated by the state; in such industries as medicine, utilities, roads, education, defence, power supply and even toilet-tissue manufacture in some places. Here we often pay for a service whether efficient or not, whether needed by us or not, with little or no option to choose.

There are exceptions to the above points and they are exceptions - not the rule. In an increasingly communications-rich world it becomes increasingly difficult and undesirable for a business of any size to disregard the morals, concerns, desires, and considerations of the society upon which it depends for that buck, whether fast or slow. And whilst I lament the way in which whole, once-untainted populations eagerly embrace some of the lowest aspects of Western culture I do not complain about their right to do so, only about the fact that aspects of their own culture and tradition have been banned or discouraged in response to global pressure for culture to fit the Western democratic corporate model.

> Guardian - May 1996
>
> # Tarmac call for 'greener' new roads
>
> **T**HE head of one of Britain's biggest road-building firms has given the Government an ultimatum that his company will not build the controversial Newbury bypass unless new environmental standards are adopted.

Most valid examples of coercive abuse from the corporate world have either passed into history, or are carried out in collusion with a state. The former are historical because the resulting publicity and public disenchantment with direct coercive action by business is damaging to their image-i.e. When the public sees a car manufacturer's hirelings shooting strikers they retaliate with their wallets. The plentiful examples of multinational and corporate abuse today exist where a corporation has enlisted the state to do the dirty work it could not do itself. Whether it is tribal people in Guatemala murdered to pursue World Bank supported dam projects, or viable communities and dwindling countryside compulsorily purchased for dubious road-building projects, it is the state with its soldiers and police who are always there to do the dirty work. The fact that two men in a garage successfully challenged the all-powerful giant, IBM, who monopolized the world computing market, speaks volumes about the vulnerability of a corporate Goliath to the power of unfettered creative competition.

We are all aware of the depths to which businesses (and people on their own) will sink in the quest for wealth, and often have personal experience of lies, deceptions and dishonouring of promises. When this has happened, when we finally recognize the deception of a business or colleague, whether in advertising or employment promises, we are in a position to stop buying the product or quit the job. However severe the disruption and inconvenience of doing this, we do not go to jail for our actions - **our desire for freedom does not result in the loss of our freedom.**

Can we really hope that the state, disconnected from the feedback loop of our society, is going to somehow make big business safer and more ethical, when we regularly witness the state exceeding the corruption of business, and often aiding and abetting its worst abuses? In the dangerous combination of big business and the state, it is the agent of the state that usually creates or officially condones the damage. Only we can protect ourselves from the dangers posed by the growth of big corporations, and the sooner we empower ourselves with this awareness the better. Because they cannot force the money from our pockets we - as their customers - have more ultimate control of their activities than does their own boardroom or the state. And in most matters of life we are able to exercise this control invisibly without the need to attend board meetings, consider too many issues or tick from limited selections in different boxes.

Disclaimer: Do not be swayed by the above propaganda. All businesses are run by evil twisted people who would sell off their grandmother if the price was right. Everything on sale anywhere is a rip-off, and you should really be making all your own stuff, from pencils to bicycles, drugs to camera film. Only then can you escape the evils of capitalism.

Guardian - May 1997

Investors taking a tougher stand on ethical issues

INVESTORS who put principles before profits are hardening their stance on a wide range of ethical issues, according to soundings taken by the Ethical Investment Research Information Service (EIRIS).

At least one in four say that, when making investment decisions, they are much more concerned about issues such as trading in arms or testing on animals then they were three years ago.

from an arms
industry
advertisement

22. The Arms Industry Toilet

The arms industry is quite often cited as a productive part of society, creating jobs, employment and exports. This is a giant hoax and as we shall see, weapons manufacture is far worse than just a useless means to create employment.

But first, have you noticed that for some forty years, the two most successful post-war economic success stories were those two countries who were forbidden to spend on arms or standing armies after the Second World War? Can it be an accident that when you do not throw a large chunk of the nation's wealth down the toilet, the rest of the economy does a lot better? Can Japan and Germany's post-war success stories have any better economic basis than this simple factor?*

*Various other factors were at play for some years, including the Marshall Plan and generous aid/investment. However, long after such factors ceased to be involved, these two economies continued to outperform their heavily armed ex-enemies.

Since the war, the victors (America, the former Soviet Union, Britain, and France) have poured huge sums into the arms industry and procured positions as suppliers of military hardware to the nations of the world. At the same time they maintain huge standing armies and a hopelessly inefficient and costly nuclear power establishment, built primarily to support their nuclear weapons programmes.

The fundamental difference between the arms industry and the majority of other commercial enterprises is that the value of military product is NEGATIVE. This is an important concept. Large sums of society's money are spent manufacturing weapon products that we hope NEVER TO USE. Assuming the weapons are not put to use, then further enormous sums are wasted looking after them, updating them, destroying old stocks and maintaining a force of people ready and willing to use them if ever ordered to do so.

Sunday Times - July 1997

US set for big arms sales

Martin Walker in Washington

PRESIDENT Clinton flew to Europe last night for the Nato enlargement summit in Madrid as the United States arms industry began to eye a potential £22 billion market in re-equipping the former eastern European countries.

And even though one country might seem to profit from selling these items to another, our global society as a whole is dragged down by the weight of their uselessness and literally torn apart if they are put to use. For, if and when these products are ever used, an even greater cost becomes apparent. When weapon products are actually used they tend to dramatically decrease the value of the products we already possess, including our lives.

The contrast with products such as the tractor, piano or sewing machine could not be greater, since these items allow us to increase the value of our lives and the world through creating food, music or clothes. We (you and me) don't buy the weaponry - it seems to be traded between a fairly exclusive club, with the end product always funded by money taken from our pockets in one country or another. Money we have justly earned with our tractor, piano and sewing machine is being **flushed down a toilet and will take us with it, if the product it paid for is ever used.**

Undoubtedly, whilst our world is run by a collection of coercively based states, we need to have what protection we can from the Hitlers, LBJ's, Pol Pots and countless others who assume leadership of nations, and with it the power to do great damage to some of us. The irony is, of course, that the biggest attraction to most would-be despots is that they can, from a position of nothing, take control of an existing state structure, complete with a tax collecting base and a population used to being under control. It might have taken centuries for this structure to develop but it can take just a few months or years for some charismatic despot to gain control.

> *"A thousand years scarce serve to form a state,*
> *An hour may lay it in the dust."*
>
> Byron, *Childe Harold's Pilgrimage (1812-28)*

The great challenge facing us now is how do we get to the condition where there is not a large powerful state waiting to be taken over. It should not be so difficult in that condition to stop future despots or fanatics from taking over and building new coercive structures to run society. There is a suggestion later on how such a condition of statelessness might be preserved once achieved.

We are told by the world's faltering great powers that their armaments buy us peace and a safe climate in which to develop our society. Yet from the examples that history has given us, it does not appear that a strong and successful arms industry and military establishment are signs of a healthy society that can endure and improve for future generations. Most of the great empires that fell did so soon after reaching their peak of strength. Yet this "who's got the biggest dick" attitude to arms acquisition is typical for the rulers of virtually any modern state. The negative economic effect of vast expenditure on arms in any society is likely to show itself as an accelerated inner decay and shift to disorder, as money that could otherwise be used productively by society is worse than wasted. It also provides for the regular re-introduction to society of those who have been trained to use guns to kill fellow human beings. When considering the total cost to us, we must include the education of those who devise new ways to kill and of the engineers who turn these ideas to production, nor forget the islands and areas of our planet that have been destroyed forever or rendered uninhabitable for millennia. We must count the loss of many precious resources of the planet and the lost productive capacity of all those producing the weaponry as well as those killed by it. Consider also the vast expanse of desert in America's Nevada where obsolete warplanes are parked wing to wing as far as the eye can see, and the mountains in nearby New Mexico that have been hollowed out to store out-dated nuclear warheads. Society simply cannot continue to suffer this expense which is meant to give us security from other countries, who buy arms so that their society is secure from us.

> Guardian - July 1997
>
> ### 'Steering' glitch for Eurofighter
>
> **F**AULTY steering and poor radar could make it impossible to fly the Eurofighter at speed and render pilots unable to identify targets properly, according to German defence experts.
> News magazine Der Spiegel
>
> the next two weeks about its commitment to order 180 of the aircraft, which is being developed with Britain, Italy and Spain. Britain is committed to buying 232, at a cost of £16 billion. Some 16,000 jobs in Lancashire, Humberside and Bristol are dependent on the project.
> A spokesman for the German defence ministry yester-

We need security but with two world wars this century, dozens of major wars and countless smaller conflicts going on all over the globe* it is apparent that our traditional approach is tragically flawed.

*We might also include the War on Drugs that helps sustain the USA military after the near evaporation of their main "enemy" - the Soviet Union.

So don't buy the argument that the weapons industry creates employment, is good for the economy, or any of that. It would almost certainly be better for our overall economy to take the vast amounts of government money spent on arms purchases, pile it into an enormous stack and set fire to it. In order to do this, or just leave the money in society in the first place, we will first need to find more innovative ways to stop the Germans, Finns or Libyans from taking over the Houses of Parliament and government of this country.* Peace will ultimately come from co-operation, freedom and an absence of the obsession with where red lines are drawn on the map; not from our possession of more and more lethal and dangerous weaponry. What could be more obvious?

* I do not wish to be flippant here and realise that some readers may insert their own neighbouring countries and have more justifiable fears.

23. Money's Real Dimension

Money and wealth are surrounded by so much emotion, envy and aspiration that we sometimes can lose touch with what money actually is, or rather what it represents. There have been volumes written on many other aspects of money - what it does, how to get it, how to manage it, invest it, etc. You would also be interested to find out just how the state, over a period of a few generations, craftily took over and debased the sound money system that society was evolving in the last century, stealing the gold in the process. It is a long and fascinating story and the nub of it was the government promise, on paper, to redeem the early bills* for gold or silver if requested. What we now call a dollar bill was once a silver certificate. A few generations after the gold and silver were taken into safekeeping by the state, the text on the notes changed and they became just a promise that they were worth a pound, dollar, so many pesos, or whatever. But though in one sense the money we now have is an artful invention of the state, it still retains a real worth as the representation of value which we create. Money is real and if we didn't have it we would have to invent it.

*As in the financial instrument, a "bill of exchange."

When a few pennies worth of clay becomes a china cup, some paint and canvas an inspiring work of art, or some silicon chips, wires and plastic become a telephone, a value has been created in the world. When one person's knowledge and experience are put to use teaching another human being to sing, or to draft watertight contracts, a value has been added to the world. Earth and Sun are converted to rice and beans by the farmer. Something that was once worth a little bit less, or very little at all, has been changed into something more valuable through the introduction of human ingenuity, intellect, and effort. We represent this value with money and it is the root source of our wealth as a society.*

*Certainly, the subject is more complex than just this. Are exhaustible resources such as oil or gold some common fund of the earth or the property of those who harvest them, often after great effort, risk and investment? Oil, of course, was discovered before the automobile and then presumably did seem as inexhaustible as sand. In some modern resorts, the beautiful sand beaches that attract tourists have been looted by builders to make the hotels in which they stay.

It is this value, or the capacity to produce it, which is enhanced and increased in money markets, then traded back and forth for gain or frequently loss. But the basis of this growing wealth is real. When the wet clay is turned into a china cup, wealth has been created, money has been made, and it has been at nobody's expense. I only make this elaborate point for those who suspect that money made is always made at the expense of somebody, somewhere else. That happens too but the value that shifts in most speculative transactions had to be created in the first place.

What a shame it is that so many of those involved in valuable and important work on this planet do so with the attitude that they should not make any money or profit from their good works. If someone, or a group of people, figure out a long-term way to alleviate world starvation, the refugee crisis, or homelessness than I, for one, wish them a healthy financial reward for their efforts. If we could get rich by saving the rainforest then more people might focus seriously on that situation.

24. Strange Fruit

It is fashionable today for politicians to try and combine the coercive power of the state with the creativity and efficiency of our enterprise culture. Unfortunately, by introducing their own coercive "do it or we'll hit you" formula into the equation, they break the feedback loop so essential for the long term success of any component of the complex system we call society.

At its most benign this combination just results in us paying them a lot to select whom we pay to do the job, as is the case with roadworks and waste handling. But the results often bear strange fruit and the very strangest of these indeed must be the wheel clamp. In the UK, "private enterprise" firms are engaged by local councils to seek out and punish vehicle owners who have parked where the state has decided they should not park. These are, presumably, places where a parked car is likely to inconvenience or endanger pedestrians or other road users. Perhaps it narrows the road by blocking a lane, or blinds vision at a dangerous corner or interferes in one way or another with safe and effective road usage. When they find someone so parked, or a parking meter tenant whose rent is overdue, they call in the clamping van which will then often double-park alongside the offending vehicle. Aware that they are creating further road blockage, the highly trained team jump out and within moments are away again, having attached a large yellow immobilising clamp onto a wheel of the car. When the driver returns, the process now required to remove the clamp takes from 30 minutes to two hours or more and costs over £ 60 ($100).*

*In Scotland in 1992 the Lord Justice General, whilst unable to pronounce on state wheel clamping, banned the practice by private landowners on the basis of his judgement that the practice was "extortion and theft."

It would seem to be obvious that the punishment for the transgression serves only to prolong the offence that has been committed, or to exacerbate the danger that is trying to be prevented. Imagine using this technique in other areas of human endeavour. You are four days late in paying the monthly rent on your apartment. As retribution the landlord locks you into your apartment for two months and demands six months rent before he will let you out. Perhaps it could be applied to drunken drivers who are forced as punishment to drink a very expensive bottle of whisky and then drive home. One could almost extend this principle to killing the friends and relatives of a convicted mass murderer.

If there is a reason not to park somewhere, then it defies common sense to punish the parker by exacerbating the offence. Yet when the state is involved, common sense is not, and combining this with private enterprise is a dangerous approach indeed.

Now we are seeing local governments rely increasingly upon fines against their constituents and confiscation of assets, to supply a basic and budgeted portion of their income. So really, if they are to fully privatise their fund-raising approach to traffic management, we should soon see some bold marketing initiatives by local traffic departments. Why not offer the motorist the opportunity to purchase five parking ticket fines in advance, and get one free, for instance! Or do a special 25% Christmas discount in December on wheel clamp removals?

In some areas the combination of state and private enterprise may indeed improve efficiency at no cost, and a case has been made for this with local council waste removal. In a well-intentioned local council, some of this saving may filter back through reduced council tax or slower increases. However, we are unlikely to share directly in the reduced cost and we are still given no choice on who removes our waste. Suppose that a company wants to start up and collect our waste for 50p a week (provided we sort it), funding their cheaper price with efficient recycling. Assuming that they could operate legally at the price of just £ 26 per year, we would most certainly still have to make our contribution to the council for waste disposal we were no longer using.

And there is no mechanism whatever in the toolbag of the state to naturally encourage less wasteful lifestyles through incentive rather than punishment. Imagine if you could develop a comfortable lifestyle that recycled almost everything, producing a bare minimum of waste that needed removal. This would be great news for the planet and your community, yet there is no direct benefit to be had through less cost for your waste removal - just the good feeling that you are in a harmonious interface with the planet.

One of the most frightening strange fruits of coercion and free enterprise is the growing privatisation of the prison industry. Here we have the state creating a private industry which relies upon the state's coercive power to supply it with inmates. This industry will always be a strong lobby in support of new laws against victimless crimes - which laws now probably account for some 70%* of all American prison inmates. Private prisons are now a "hot" investment stock in America, which has seen its prison population triple over a twenty year period during which crimes involving victims have remained essentially constant.

> * This is a fair guess, based on the established 60% that are drug offenders and assuming that another 10% are made up from the plethora of other victimless crime offences that can land you in an American jail these days, including making errors on or not submitting business forms completed for statistical purposes.

The coercive "do it or I'll hit you" approach has never been a successful long-term strategy for businesses, companies or enterprises. Attempting to harness this approach with private enterprise in order to make the state more efficient brings very grave dangers with only an occasional cost saving benefit.

Los Angeles Times Service
LOS ANGELES — A Los Angeles County parking control officer who ticketed a Cadillac parked illegally got no backtalk from the driver sitting stiffly at the steering wheel.

The driver was dead, shot in the head perhaps 13 hours earlier, county sheriff's investigators said. Yet, the civilian parking officer left the ticket inside the car, on the dashboard, and drove off without contacting the authorities.

"He was noticeably dead," said Paul Hatherly, a county paramedic. "The driver's window was three-quarters down. He had severe rigor mortis. He was discolored."

"I think it could be plausibly argued that changes of diet are more important than changes of dynasty or even of religion."

George Orwell, 1937

"The Road to Wigan Pier"

Launched by the author in 1982

25. Meat of the Issue

We hear a lot about meat and the abuse of animals today from various groups who see this as a major moral problem facing mankind. As the originator of the VegeBurger®, I do understand where they are coming from but, from a very different viewpoint, it has seemed to me for some time that we are perhaps doing "domestic animals" a favour by including them in our food chain. I just don't think we should do them this favour, because the price we have to pay is too high. And I doubt the issue would be a problem were the state not so intricately involved at the primary end of our food chain. The interface that has developed (in the West) with domestic animals bears all the hallmarks of a classic host-parasite relationship.

In this relationship it is quite plausible to view man as the host and the domestic animals as the parasites. Though we need not envy the lifestyle of the average chicken or cow, they have, together with sheep and pigs, done extraordinarily well on the evolutionary ladder as species. They have multiplied and flourished. In us, they have a host who diligently covers over 70% of his arable land in crops designed NOT to be eaten by humans, but to be fed to domestic animals. They are eating our basic food resource. Whilst we are unable to adequately house our own species, vast acres of the country are covered in buildings built for the sole benefit of domestic animals, who must ultimately pay the bill with their sorry lives.

What do we get in return, other than worldwide malnutrition and starvation due to this huge parasitic bite out of the food chain? Disease and food poisoning is the simple answer. The excessive consumption of animal products, made possible by state subsidies and the factory farm, has now been implicated in virtually every major degenerative disease of the West, and is the source of over 90% of food poisoning cases - a ris-

jan 1989

THREE million people will suffer from salmonella poisoning this year in the estimation of one of our foremost bacteriologists.

True, the symptom for the great majority of them will be no more than a nasty tummy ache. The Government's Principal Medical Officer speaks of it as an epidemic.

The Ministry of Agriculture disagrees. Only about 26 people have died of salmonella poisoning in the last 12 months, so they can ing epidemic. Did you know that massive subsidies are paid out so makers of animal feed can buy cereals at prices much cheaper than those paid by flour millers or makers of breakfast cereal for human consumption? Do you know anyone who ever marched or lobbied under the "Cheap Food For Cows" banner? Yet we pay dearly with both our wallets and our health, to support this state intervention and control of our food chain.

I am not questioning whether it is moral or immoral to raise animals to kill and eat. I am saying we are being taken for a ride and that it is foolhardy in the extreme to destroy the natural flora and fauna of the countryside to support a handful of intensively farmed crops that are then fed to a handful of animal species to produce subsidised meat at the expense of the quality and price of our primary food sources. Our return on this mad investment in meat is from a quarter to a tenth of the nutrients that we put into it - and we eat our food second-hand.

Perhaps there is a defensible argument to be made for rearing animals on the naturally occurring food waste of ingredients (like cereal husks) that we cannot digest ourselves, or for putting domestic animals to graze in some of the areas where crop farming is not feasible. Though I am not making this argument,* it is true that these animals would not have a life or be widespread as a species were they not part of the human food agenda (the same is true of wheat and cabbages). Without the subsidies that come straight from our pockets anyway, the price of animal products and meat would rise to a price reflecting the real cost of production-which is considerable.** Meat consumption would fall to the level of an occasional foodstuff rather than the mainstay of our diet, a position it only attained a few generations ago due to state support, and one which does not prevail in most of the world even today - and never can without the accessory of mass starvation for humans as other mammals feed at our own primary food source.

*My personal belief is that it is a sordid and ungrateful practice to kill our fellow mammals for food. But we have been eating meat, albeit in small amounts, as part of our diet for most of our time on earth. I would far rather see a slow drift away from meat consumption as acceptable social behaviour over a hundred years, than to have those running the state proclaim bans and create new squadrons of police to enforce animal rights. Their numbers and powers would only grow as more and more abuse took place, pet disappearances needed investigation, clandestine restaurants needed busting and so on.

** Howard Lyman, food director of the U.S. Humane society, claimed in the Guardian that the average American hamburger would cost $11 were there no subsidy structure for US beef.

Without the central interference by the growing European state in our food chain, we would never have produced the vast surplus of unwanted beef that some inspired bureaucrat thought would be clever to feed back to the vegetarian cattle from which it came. Is this how these clever people had temporarily reduced the notorious frozen beef mountain? Never in a free market situation could the laws of economics be so twisted that an industry feeds its finished product back to itself as a raw ingredient. It is like going to all the trouble of making a new road-ready car, knowing that you will promptly scrap it to use the recovered junk metal as the raw ingredient of your next production.

Today's continuing drift away from focused red meat consumption and towards more vegetable foods in the diet is accompanied by a growing appreciation of the mental and physical health benefits to be achieved thereby. Yet despite our shifting diet we are still being charged to support the wholesale rape of our countryside in order to keep our larders filled with regular doses of cheap meat and animal foods.

And don't be misled by the foolish question of "what do we do with all the animals if people stop eating them." We put them back on their natural place in the food chain, for those who wish to indulge in pre-eaten food, and stop putting them up in cheap hotels feeding them mass-produced junk food. By relieving the pressure to devote every acre to agriculture, we allow back some of the natural wild mammals, small animals and birds that used to share this land with us, and that now exist most securely only where there is income to be made from hunting them. It is a shocking state of affairs when the wild animals of the country begin moving into the city for safety, as are foxes, falcons, wood pigeons and other species.

> Guardian - Nov 1996
>
> # Crisis plan to get farmers out of beef
>
> FARMERS hit by the beef crisis may be retrained to grow crops or take up alternative employment under contingency plans being prepared by the Government.
>
> *(the Lord help them! Author note)*

Just let the meat industry be part of the real world of material costs, supply, demand and product liability to which every other business must attune itself; meat would then be dethroned from its improper place at the top of our food chain and restored to the quality and safety that prevailed for our occasionally meat-eating ancestors.

"The Drug War is fuelled by the fact that at this historic moment...our politicians are suffering from enemy deprivation. Faced with the real problems of urban decay, slipping global competitiveness, and a deteriorating educational system, the government has decided instead to turn its energies toward the sixty million Americans who use illegal psychoactive drugs."

Timothy Leary

26. The Drugs Problem

The primary problem with drugs is that they are illegal and/or state-controlled. This counter-evolutionary control by the state, of substances that we take for other than nutritional purposes, is the root cause of virtually all the problems that people are concerned about in connection with drugs, drug abuse, and drug-related crime. Sure, all drugs have potential problems if abused. But we are human beings, and able to make judgements about these things, and treat them with respect and caution - just as we must with our food. Most drug users treat new drugs with respect, taking a small dose to ascertain their reaction. If people do not like the effect of cannabis or LSD upon them, then they are unlikely to become regular users.

It should not surprise us that young people, especially, seek to experiment with drugs that alter or enhance their perception of life, and that youths and adults seek a drug-granted respite from the predictability of everyday life. There's a menu full of options out there to choose from but - surprise surprise - the only legal way to get out of your head is with alcohol. The biggest cause of alcoholism is the non-availability on the market of the numerous safer, non-addictive and less befuddling alternatives, cannabis in particular. Alcohol consumption is dropping significantly amongst Europe's youth, together with football hooliganism, as a wider selection of drugs becomes available. It seems a reasonable desire for people to find some means to get "out of their heads" from time to time - to take a totally different perspective on life. Perhaps some new perspectives on life are needed in the world today and the attraction to drugs is evolution trying to happen. We should be pleased that today's generation is avoiding the trap of alcohol addiction, together with the anti-social behaviour, depression, trivia worship, and middle-age burnout that abusers risk. Used sensibly, alcohol can be a beneficial drug that enhances and maintains our health and well-being. Alcohol has a well-earned place in our culture but that place should not be defended by state legislation and turned into a drug monopoly.

Drugs are a part of us and our culture and as most of us learned in school, drugs often formed the core of the early business which brought the world's differing cultures into trade with each other. These products of trade included tobacco, alcohol, opium, tea,* coffee, chocolate, cocaine and sugar.** We could almost regard pepper and spices as virtual drugs to the taste buds of the bland European palate of the mid-millennium. The glorious history of trade in the civilized world relied upon civilization's search for new and diverse drugs and sensory input. People have always sought to include drugs in their diets for many non-medical reasons: whether to stay awake longer, or to fall asleep quicker; whether to drown their sorrows or to better understand them; whether to enjoy a banter in the bar with friends, or have mystic communication with a tree; whether to explore their dark side or say hello to the God within them. Some drugs are not an escape from "reality" but a gateway to exploring the very nature of reality. Even the humble drug tea was first discovered by Buddhist monks who valued it to help them stay up all night meditating in order to get high. One could imagine how dismayed they would be by casual tea abuse in modern Britain.

*Tea was such an expensive 18th century American drug that its affluent users would eat the buttered and salted dried leaves after having boiled them into a strong bitter brew. (James Trager, The Foodbook, Grossman NY)

**Prior to the discovery of sugar cane, the primary sweetening for European culture had been expensive honey available from bees that were, of course, not fed sugar. Sugar has the habit-forming effect of raising our blood-sugar level rapidly to a degree useable only by someone running the 100 metre dash. Our blood sugar level drops soon after this rush, leading to a craving for more.

Some of the banned drugs are not just less dangerous than alcohol - they are hardly dangerous at all and can lead to behaviour which could quite possibly be downright good for the individual and society. Cannabis, LSD and psilocybin mushrooms have not even got an annual death toll of one apiece. Ecstasy (MDMA) kills fewer people each

> Sunday Times Dec 1996
>
> # Judges shift towards legalising soft drugs
>
> Leading judges have revealed for the first time they want to see soft drugs and prostitution within licensed brothels decriminalised.

year than does aspirin, lightning hits, or beef consumption. And millions of happy users continue to use these drugs with far less damage than that experienced by alcohol drinkers, amphetamine abusers, cocaine sniffers, cigarette puffers or chocolate box gobblers. There is some risk - all drugs carry some risk if abused, even aspirin. But if we wish to enjoy the benefits, then we have to accept the responsibility, just as we take care when we get in our car or on our bike and take to the roads, or check to see how fresh the food is at a self-service restaurant. Much of our life consists of balancing the risks in life with the benefits to be had.

Getting happy, loving, insightful, bursting with positive energy, able to dance all night or just chilled out, are all definitely nice things to do and I say boo to the prigs who claim that these valuable experiences are invalid when we make use of a drug to assist us in getting to a desired state of mind. Let them keep drinking their instant coffee, using one-hour film processors, flying across the world in hours instead of weeks. Let them eat their frozen dinners, sliced pre-baked bread and take-away fast food, working on computers that can do millions of calculations per second. Let them tune into instant escape from reality on a multitude of TV channels; but accessing happiness, peace, boundless energy or deep feelings of love quickly and without great expense? Oh no, this must be done the long way through years of grief and hard work; or purchased, if we are to believe the advertising, when you select the right brand of automobile, sanitary towel, or soft drink.

Contrast the state's complacency regarding what we put into our bodies under the guise of food with its concern against what we ingest to feed our heads (an apt phrase from the Sixties). With food, that basic and essential necessity of life, we can do just about anything we like, eating whatever we like for any reason whenever we want to. We are allowed to consume chemical food additives that have no natural equivalent on planet Earth. The state even assures us that all this stuff is safe, as they did with every now-banned additive when it was still legal. We are allowed to eat genetically modified foodstuffs - the like of which could only have evolved in nature had you persuaded and enabled a scorpion to mate with a tomato. We can freely consume four times as much food as we need, and more than our body can safely deal with. We can go on doing this as long as we please, consuming beef-burgers and soft drinks all the way to our state-provided hospital death-bed if we so choose. In the early 1990's the American Surgeon General attributed 80% of all illness-related deaths to diet-related causes. Yet nobody will jail you anywhere in the world for eating yourself to death.

So who is protecting whom from what? How can the state have the effrontery to control and legislate what we do with our own state of mind? Just what is going on here? Literally, you can go to jail for puffing on a plant that makes you feel happy and loving, gives you no crunching hangover, and is safer than crossing the road.

Cannabis is the most risk-free illegal drug in existence, with a recognized safe history going back thousands of years. It is a much happier and safer alternative to alcohol without the effect of making users befuddled and arrogant. If someone's reaction to cannabis is likely to impair their ability to drive, they realize that they are not safe behind a wheel, and driving is the last thing they want to do in that condition - unlike the drunk who is convinced that he can take on the whole world with total competence. As far as I know, there is no statistical data linking cannabis consumption with actual dangerous driving. Cannabis is a drug and use can turn to abuse and lead to reduced focus and motivation; this is a risk that is easier for a pot user to deal with when it occurs than it is for an alcohol user. And if it does occur, it is usually when cannabis is taken in combination with the addictive drug, tobacco. You are more likely to hear pure smokers talk about getting high, and tobacco mixers about getting stoned.

Cannabis smoking was never perceived as a big problem, or associated with crime, until the 1930's when Harry Anslinger, the fanatically ambitious head of America's first federal drug agency, launched his Cannabis-Killer Drug campaign. He had the full backing and support of publishing baron William Randolph Hearst and a bunch of his timber-owning buddies to back this push to wipe out hemp cultivation. It was the threat of cannabis to undermine his timber to paper industry that motivated the press magnate* to give his backing to Anslinger. The movie "REEFER MADNESS," a piece of baseless anti-cannabis propaganda, was shown to almost every

All leading independent research has come to the same general conclusion that Cannabis "...in its natural form is one of the safest therapeutically active substances known to man" (Findings of Senior USA DEA ADMINISTRATIVE LAW JUDGE Francis Young). Also "...there are no known cases of death in humans from Cannabis...."(The Pharmaceutical Journal Vol 254 No.6843 pp772). In comparison Tobacco is attributed to over 100,000 deaths each year in the UK. Alcohol, which is responsible for over 30,000 deaths each year is also implicated in 60-70% of homicides, 75% of stabbings and 50% of domestic assaults (1989 BMA report findings).

(From The Lancet Editorial Nov 11, 1995)

child, teacher and parent in America and shaped the country's attitude to drug use. Its legacy still fuels groundless fears that lead to continued suppression of a substance widely recognized as harmless. The thousands of hemp farmers of America had to change crops or go bust.

*The cannabis plant, hemp, can produce up to four times as much paper per acre as trees, and was the first US agricultural product ever referred to as a "billion dollar" crop - in a 1938 "Popular Mechanics" article, which read: "...a machine has been invented which solves a problem more than 6000 years old. The machine is designed for removing the fibre-bearing cortex from the rest of the stalk, making hemp fibre available for use without a prohibitive amount of human labour. Hemp is the standard fibre of the world...and can be used to produce more than 25,000 products ranging from dynamite to cellophane." The fictitious dangers of cannabis smoking were used as the excuse to virtually destroy the hemp industry and stave off the threat to the paper mills Hearst and his friends owned. At the same time DuPont and the nylon industry were ready to launch their alternative synthetic ropes and fibres. Hemp was the world's largest agricultural crop from 1000 BC until 1883 AD and made our earliest example of woven fabric (8000-7000BC). It has a long history of effective use in medicine. Getting safely "high" is just a minor fringe benefit that this wonderfully useful plant offers our culture. (from Herer's book "The Emperor Wears No Clothes.")

The growing range of drugs referred to as psychedelics all have their original roots and inspirations in natural substances that our species has used for millennia in the search for altered consciousness and greater understanding of the nature of God and the universe. The state bans these substances for the same reason that they issue passports and control which borderlines we cross. Psychedelics are the travelling drugs - they do not, generally speaking, work by stimulating or reducing urges or inhibitions. They are not addictive, have a very high lethal dose if any, and account for barely a handful of fatalities per annum. They take us into a different place - we travel to other dimensions, or see new dimensions in the world around us. In many ways the familiar world we live in, with brick houses, plumbers, parliaments, radios, cars, roads, suits, restaurants and so forth is but one channel on the set of all possible channels. Because this is the "reality" we have created within the world around us we are tuned to it to such a degree that we can easily become oblivious to the deeper nature of the vast Universe that encompasses the little fleck of matter in space we call Earth.

Psychedelics are not taken as an "escape" from this world but as a ticket to see it from a different perspective, even from a different dimension. It is hard to emerge from this voyage without developing a realization, amongst many others, that those "in power" are possessed of a narrow vision fuelled primarily by the desire to stay in power. Their viewpoint is of one channel only - the one that represents the status quo in whatever country they control - and their efforts to fine-tune this channel to a micro degree can often appear ludicrous. Thus, these drugs reveal clearly that "the emperor has no clothes" and must be prohibited at all costs.

Many of the psychedelics grow naturally on this planet and have been utilised from the early days of our species along with the other gifts of the Earth that we use to feed, clothe and heal ourselves. Their popularity, and their undeserved illegalisation has led to a growth in man-made alternatives such as LSD, Ecstasy, and 2CB; substances which are themselves routinely banned as soon as it becomes apparent that yet another means to acquire a passport has been found, another door opened. Unlike experiences with tobacco, alcohol, chocolate or heroin, you rarely find cannabis or psychedelic users who continue to take these drugs whilst professing a constant desire to quit taking them. Psychedelics should always be treated with respect - sometimes they give their own stern reminders when this is not done.

Not all drugs are as safe and non-addictive as cannabis. Some, like heroin, cocaine, and controlled pharmaceuticals, carry serious risks and can create dependency and addiction. These are routinely made illegal in the belief that this will reduce consumption. The evidence could not be more to the contrary. Both the organised drugs dealers and police forces grow in strength and stand to make more money or preside over bigger budgets in an illegal drugs climate. Products are sold without identification, industry controls, manufacturer name, usage instructions, safety cautions, or any buyer's guarantee or maker's liability. In a free market, the legal liabilities for makers of crack cocaine could be a lot more frightening and inhibiting than the ineffective drugs squad.

In a free and informed drugs market fewer would choose the dangerous drugs, and the evidence in the UK and Holland supports this, as the majority of drug users choose the far less toxic cannabis and psychedelics. Many of these users have sampled drugs such as heroin, crack cocaine, amphetamines or alcohol and simply not become regular users. People are able to make intelligent choices and when they are enjoying life they are naturally interested in preserving their own, and act accordingly. Yet the state steadfastly refuses to let us exercise our own judgement in drug use. We live in a world where if you choose to make up your own mind about what you do with it, you can go to jail - for your own good of course.

This crazy attitude has embroiled most of the world in a virtual Third World War under the guise of America's internationally exported War on Drugs. Whole economies have been ravaged, and vast sums are spent each year from our taxes and confiscated from our citizens, while the numbers imprisoned worldwide must equal the annual casualties of a great ongoing war. This Third World War does not defend us from some great Evil threatening society and serves no useful purpose but to fatten the coffers of those waging it - from the countless worldwide bureaus, agencies and police forces, to the ever-expanding prison industry and makers of testing apparatus. Perhaps the zeal with which this new war is waged reflects the state's own dependency on the massive tax revenues it raises from the approved drugs, and hinges on its cosy, centuries-long relationship with distillers, tobacco companies and the pharmaceutical industry - the biggest drug dealers in the world.* Another prime stimulus to this war arises from religious bigots who fear that personal revelations of brotherhood and oneness with God might not be in strict accordance with church teachings, and could thus bypass the need for a priesthood to interpret these higher matters for us.

*The term drug dealer is used in a descriptive and not pejorative sense.

The casualties of this war on drugs are many and varied. Most obvious are the hundreds of thousands of our world's citizens who are locked up, at our expense,* for indulging or trading in alternatives to the standardized "OK by the USA" drugs - substances such as alcohol, tobacco, Prozac, prescription sedatives, coffee, and cola drinks that must be the only mood or mind-altering fare available to the world. Though it is openly acknowledged that the majority of illegal drug shipments do get through to their markets, the casualties and costs continue to mount with no benefit for society.

*It is estimated to cost about $400,000 to put a single (USA) drug dealer in jail; composed of $150,000 to arrest and convict, $50,000-$150,000 for an additional prison bed and an average five years in jail at a cost of $30,000 per annum.

Another level of casualties in this war evolves from the distortion of the natural market, which drives people to take more dangerous drugs than they would choose in a free market. The laws banning cannabis cultivation and use carry more responsibility for the growth of crack cocaine than do all the cocaine barons of Columbia put together. They also carry responsibility for solvent related deaths, teenage alcoholism,

madness from Datura (Jimson weed), and other aspects of the drug
problem than does any other single factor. Though there is justified
outrage at the probable part played by the CIA in the introduction of
crack cocaine to America's inner cities, the statistics would suggest
that the War on Drugs itself is the largest causative factor of America's
downhill slide into dangerous drug abuse. According to NIDA research
for the USA, tobacco and alcohol kill twice as many people in a week

GROWTH OF DRUG PRISONERS IN U.S. JAILS

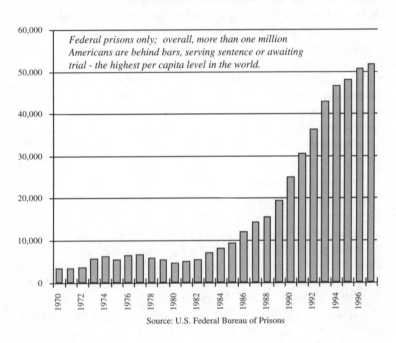

*Federal prisons only; overall, more than one million
Americans are behind bars, serving sentence or awaiting
trial - the highest per capita level in the world.*

Source: U.S. Federal Bureau of Prisons

as do all illegal drugs combined in a year.* Unlike alcohol and tobacco,
cannabis is neither addictive nor credited with any deaths per annum;
and do not forget the millions dependent upon prescribed pharmaceuticals with damaging, often lethal side-effects, who for some reason are
excluded altogether from the "drug problem" statistics.

*Deaths per annum in the USA: tobacco 390,000; alcohol 80,000; cocaine 2200,
heroin 2000, cannabis 0, others 300.

This war has clogged courts and jails worldwide with drug cases.

The U.S.A. has 2.8% of its adult population (5% of adult males) in jail. This is the highest incarceration rate in the world and three times the world average. America's Stalinistic forfeiture laws against drug users now routinely provide budgeted income to local state agencies as they seize valuable property, boats and businesses of people accused of being in the drugs trade - before their cases have even been tried in court! Even when proven innocent, it is difficult, costly and time-consuming to recover forfeited property. It seems evident that the War on Drugs creates far more problems than drugs ever posed on their own.

Like the American Prohibition of alcohol in the 1920's this surreptitious World War Three has no chance whatsoever of success. As we know from history, the effect of Prohibition was to double the overall level of alcohol consumption, increase deaths from badly made alcohol, and give the Mafia a very successful start in life, with a database of almost every club, bar or place of entertainment in the USA. The whole effort was an excellent example of the "terminal toolbag" in action.

We do have a problem with young people taking drugs as well as with middle aged and elderly people. It is a very serious problem that is getting worse. For some reason, though, the perception of this problem is focused entirely on the very small range of drugs which are being used illegally. Why do we ignore the vast problems faced by those who are using drugs prescribed by doctors, and whose lives are messed-up and sometimes destroyed as a result either of doctor error, their own abuse of the prescribed stocks,* or just years of being addicted to synthetic pharmaceuticals with known side-effects? These can only be obtained through controlled channels but these channels translate into a multi-billion dollar industry throughout the world - the real drugs trade. The most successful drugs are those such as steroids, beta blockers and antihistamines which do not cure, but instead create a life-long habit for the user, often translating to hundreds of dollars or

> Guardian - Oct 1996
>
> ## Legislation fails to curb drug abuse
>
> **T**OUGH national policies on drug users may be no more effective in cutting crime than those which are more lenient, experts working for the European Union's new monitoring centre said yesterday.
>
> The centre's first annual report on the state of the drugs problem across the 15 member states concludes that the use of drugs, particularly hard drugs, is rare, but that users form between a third and 40 per cent of Europe's prison population.

pounds a month. These drug dealers openly lobby and encourage the state to pass laws controlling and restricting the alternative healing industry in the sale of herbal and other natural medicinal remedies. Even the deadly killers alcohol and tobacco are usually blinkered out of the vision when the vast majority talk about "the drug problem."

*Ecstasy users, for example, tend not to have a month's supply in a bottle.

Guardian - 16 apr 1996

Study reveals cures that kill

BAD reactions to prescribed medicines could be a leading cause of death in the United States, behind only heart disease, cancer and strokes, according to a new study...

The article reveals that from 76,000 to 137,000 people died and a further 2.2 million required hospital treatment. Such figures are not recorded in the U.K.

While acknowledging the dangers posed by some illegal drugs, I point out that the unnecessary suffering and destruction meted out by the "authorized" drugs trade is clearly the greater problem, despite being managed by trained people in white coats and slick PR professionals. More people will almost surely die from mis-applied or mis-prescribed pharmaceuticals in a month, probably even in a week, than from the so-called "drug problem" in a year. The statistics are not released and possibly not even tallied.

Disclaimer: Readers are advised to avoid all illegal drugs and to only ever ingest those substances that have been approved by the government, or prescribed by a government-approved doctor. Then you will be a happy, healthy bunny.

Guardian - Nov 1996

Million accidents a year

MORE than 1 million people a year are injured in accidents in NHS hospitals, three quarters of them patients, says the National Audit Office in a report published today.

Arrangements in many hospitals do not comply with the health and safety laws, and a

PROHIBITION THROUGH THE AGES

16th Century	Coffee banned in Egypt and supplies of coffee burned - use spreads rapidly
17th Century	The scar of Russia executes tobacco users
c.1650	Tobacco prohibited in Bavaria, Saxony, Zurich; the Ottoman sultan zealously executes smokers to no avail.
1736	The Gin Act fails to halt consumption in England.
1845	New York bans the public sale of liquor - repeals law two years later.
1875-1914	27 states and cities ban opium smoking-consumption increases sevenfold.
1914	U.S. Congress passes Harrison Narcotics Act controlling opium and cocoa derivatives.
1914-1970	Congress passes 55 laws to strengthen Harrison Act
1918	Special Committee studies Harrison Act effects-widespread smuggling .and increased use of narcotics-and calls for stricter enforcement.
1919	Prohibition laws ban alcohol consumption in USA - consumption doubles.
1919-1933	Use of marijuana, ether, and coffee increases.
1924	U.S. Congress bans heroin completely-and heroin replaced morphine in blackmarket.
1937	First U.S. Federal law passed against marijuana use.
1949	Law enforcement crackdown on non-prescription barbiturates-use increases 800% from 1942-1969.
1958	Soviets raise alcohol prices 23% to reduce consumption - policy fails.
1959	Concerted campaign against glue sniffing begins-causes "a boom in cocaine smuggling" by 1969.
1962	The FDA stops legal production of LSD - LSD use skyrockets by 1970.
1965	Amphetamine use crackdown further stimulates importation of cocaine.
1968	Campaign against marijuana use among troops in Vietnam prompts growing heroin use.
1969	New York city arrests 9000 more for drug use with no impact on drug availability & use.
1971	All-out campaign against heroin use in Vietnam fails.
1971	900 pounds of heroin seized in New York City has no impact on price.
1971	President Nixon declares drugs "America's public enemy No.1"
1972	U.S.A. passes a $1 Billion anti-drug bill.
1973	Rockefeller passes another tough anti-drug bill in New York
1973	President Nixon declares "We have turned the corner on drug .addiction in America."
1973	Singapore sets death penalty for drug trafficking -a few years later a drug official admits that "Heroin seems to be more widely used than ever."
1977	Bar Association concludes that Rockefeller Bill has had no effect on heroin consumption.
1980	300,000 youths in Malaysia estimated to be using illegal drugs.
1987	Malaysia's 12-foot high security fence along border with Thailand fails to stop drug traffic.
1987	Soviets increase penalties against moonshining in bid to lower alcohol use.
1987	Soviet legal alcohol production down 30%; moonshining up 40%; home-made wine production up 300%; 200,000 prosecuted for illegal home brewing.
1988	U.S. Senate adds $2.6 billion to federal anti-drug efforts.
1989	Ronald Reagan declares victory in War on Drugs as being his major achievement.
1989	U.S. Secretary of State reports that the global war on narcotics "is clearly not being won."
1990-1997	America exports its war on drugs worldwide - drug consumption increases worldwide. How long must this continue???

Courtesy of the Cato Institute - via *The Emperor Wears No Clothes* - ISBN 09524560 01

1999	DRUG WAR ENDS?

LAST STAND OF THE BLOODY REGIME
Daily Express 9 Oct 1989

HARD-LINE East Germany is today on the brink of a political explosion which could undermine one of the toughest Communist regimes in the world.

Police yesterday sealed off the Gethsemane church in East Berlin after more than 3,000 people attended a service for political prisoners and protesters detained in mass demonstrations at the weekend.

Last night heavily-equipped riot police surrounded the church and ordered the crowd to disperse.

VICTORY FOR ACID HOUSE POLICE
Daily Express *(same issue as above)*

DRUG-BUSTING police sealed off an entire town twice at the weekend to claim their first victory over the Acid House cult.

Six thousand revellers were turned back from Chatham, Kent, in the early hours of yesterday after a specially trained squad of 250 officers outmanoeuvred them across three counties.

Then, yesterday afternoon, a second attempt was made to stage the huge party. Up went the road blocks again and whole convoys of cars were turned back. The Express was there to report the victory exclusively.

27.   A New Church

Every weekend in Great Britain, half a million or more people gather in places of worship and joyfully celebrate their humanity and love for one another. Some of them came to know each other socially or in business and more have met through attendance at the church. Many of them take the sacrament and many just partake of the holiness of the time and place as a "holiday" from the stresses of the harder and sometimes joyless world of work and material matters.

The church I am speaking about has no central organisation and no published doctrine. There is no one to worship in this church but God in whatever form the churchgoers perceive the universal concept. This new church takes many forms, and gatherings can be located in empty warehouses, purpose-built venues, open fields, on the beach or wherever circumstances lead. Geographically, it is not even certain whether this free-form religion began in England, the Balearic Islands or the Indian subcontinent. This will be for historians to determine. What is certain is that it has spread rapidly throughout Europe, Australia, N.Z., Japan, parts of South America, and now begins to blossom in that last bastion of change, the U.S.A.

The church goes by many names and here I will simply call it the New Party. I do this because the new devotees often refer to "going to a party" when they are planning their worship, though nothing in the history of partying has ever been the same. The celebration is of life, love and harmonies. One of the tangible aspects of this church's atmosphere is described by the term "safe" - the "cool" of the Nineties. The New Parties are not meat markets though an abundance of meeting takes place. Indeed, through these parties, today's generation is re-inventing the community, a valuable social tool that has become an increasingly endangered tradition over the last few decades. Many of us today are more up-to-date with the surrogate lives of our favourite TV soap opera characters than with the real-life events that move and shake our neighbours and our workmates.

The community, a low budget and sustainable alternative to the "jet-set" of the 50's, is constantly on the move, travelling to well-established sites such as Ibiza, Byron Bay, Goa, and total eclipses - regularly moving between European cities for annual parties and special events in Berlin, Hamburg, Prague, London, Wales, Normandy, Sarajevo, or an oak forest in Portugal. Today party-goers and DJ's move fluidly around the globe, secure in the knowledge that they have a community in many parts of the world which will know, understand and welcome them.

Central to the new church is the new music, techno - as much a departure from all that came before it as were the Beatles and Pink Floyd to Frank Sinatra and Glen Miller. This new music is as difficult to digest and understand for many of the Rock n' Roll generation as rock music was to their parents, but it is essential to the ritual of the dance and the nature of the party that it supports. It is pure music that works with rhythms and beats, made by musicians who work with computers as well as instruments, sampled sounds and dedicated new technology. Some of this dedicated equipment is as essential to the new music as was the invention of the piano machine to Back and Beethoven. Nearly a century of English-language dominance of the worldwide popular music industry threatens now to be overturned, as music begins, once again, to be held more important than the lyric or the performer's personality. It is music to take your mind where you like, with an absence of complex lyrics or story lines. It is music to dance through the night with.

In the last ten years, the family tree of techno has spawned an awesome array of musical styles continually re-attuning to millions of different ears as those ears are being moved by the music's evolution. Different branches of this tree produce different styles of party. Most parties will incorporate a chill-out area, where slower and softer ambient music is played while the celebrants relax between dances, catch up with friends, or chill for most of the whole night. Though many parties are at regular venues, the cream of them will usually be produced by party-teams who seek to deliver the "best party ever" to most of those present, creating the finest mix of music, ambiance and sound quality ever experienced. And they are successful surprisingly often. The positive collaboration and positive competition to inspire the cosmic punters make for some great parties, and they are probably the safest form of "youth entertainment" this century. You are more likely to suffer injury or death down at the pub, disco, out sailing, whilst riding to hounds, or going for a swim.

The closest thing to the preacher of the old-style fixed beliefs church, or the rock star of the old music industry, is today's DJ, who draws people to a party because of his or her skill at getting the music right - being the vibrant pulse of the party, moving with it and being moved by it. Yet few of those who follow a DJ to a party would recognize them on the bus, or wish to have posters of them, or autographs. The same is true of the musicians and the bands they form - they are known and loved for their music and not their personalities and PR hype. Techno maestros don't do chat shows.

As with some religions, there is a sacrament often taken at these parties, in the form of specific drugs - substances the same as or very like those taken at some of the earliest religious ceremonies recorded from different faiths. Some will take psilocybin mushrooms, reputed by Terence McKenna to be the original "flesh of Christ" in the Christian sacrament. Others will partake of LSD, MDMA (Ecstasy), cannabis, other drugs, and sometimes a tin or two of beer. Many celebrants will take no drugs at all and just partake of the spirit that is tangibly present. Cocaine use is infrequent, and amphetamine use would reduce were reputable Ecstasy and other preferred substances more readily available.

Dance is the ritual - a celebratory and traditional form of worship that releases tensions of the week and promotes physical healing. The positive effects of the dance probably more than offset any toxic elements that might be present in some of the drugs taken. The dance, too, is new and does not depend upon a partner. You may be part of a possé, or with your partner, but it need not be evident to anyone else. If the participants lay claim to any religion in particular, it is probably that of paganism for they are likely to see God in every aspect of creation, from the babbling brook to the tree, mountain, or swallow flying overhead - and particularly in their fellow human beings.

It is a church of personal enlightenment and revelations that are shared and compared rather than delivered from a pulpit by some demagogue who is more than likely recounting the handed-down and sanitised account of someone else's revelation from a distant past in a very different society. It might be true that in the return from the enlightenment experience the drug user "brings back" less of the revelation than does the monk who spent twenty years on the path, but much of great value is brought back and filtered and refined through the process of discussion and reflec-

> *"We can be knowledgable with other men's knowledge but we cannot be wise with other men's wisdom."*
>
> *Montaigne (1533 - 1592)*

tion. And it is first-hand experience, not just recounted wisdom, however deep. To enlighten according to Collins Dictionary, is to "give information or understanding" and "to free from prejudice, superstition, etc." We can use some of that.

The members of this community serve each other, making and selling to each other clothes, music, jewellery, food, drugs, artwork, and many items of the culture at festivals, shops, or across cafe tables around the world. Much of this economy tends to provide a lower than average level of financial support to the countless faces of the state needing feeding - the Dept. of This or That, the Bureaucracy of Brussels, parliaments, the military-industrial complex, foreign "aid," prison construction, etc. and seems well able to look after itself without this added burden. This largely small-scale and free-floating new enterprise structure could be seen as a sort of New Age business community, where good karma and a sound reputation count for a lot. And it should be encouraged, not through any state subsidy, but through lack of attack by the tax-greedy authorities and the chieftains of the War on Drugs. What is perhaps feared most is that the new community questions some of the basic principles that the authorities would legislate as the foundation of our culture - the altar stones of material greed, taxes, conflict, and respect for authority.

At a more instinctive level, the custodians of order know that dramatic revelations on a personal level, whether acquired through years of meditation and study, or through an interface with the cosmic intelligence of the universe, have one inevitable result if allowed to flourish - they change our society and culture. The would-be controllers see their job as keeping things stable, by which they mean keeping them the way they are now, or rather the way they would like it to be now, or maybe the way they imagine things used to be some time in the past, when society seemed to work better. They don't really know what they want, but new ideas and trends certainly set their alarm bells ringing, because they only know how to control what they know. This is why the established order of the day persecuted the early Christians; why, in 1600, Giordano Bruno was burnt to death by Christians for maintaining that the Earth was not the centre of the Universe; and why, in 1966, the American Food & Drug Administration burned the books of a Japanese teacher who suggested that the American diet did not promote good health.*

*Georges Ohsawa on macrobiotics

It would seem appropriate that, at a time when the planet itself is threatened, a community should develop that is able to glimpse and thereby respect the glory of the universal spirit in everything it infuses, rather than just in the image and likeness of our own arrogant selves.

The new church, party, call it what you like, is evolution happening - meeting the needs of our society and filling some of the gaps that the old generation traditionally complain about. It has happened quietly enough on the fringes of society and without the benefit of PR companies or listings in events guides. The church has managed to grow large with a low profile. It is a church that takes great joy in the wondrousness of being - of life itself. In the Middle Ages, its participants would have been burnt as witches or persecuted out of existence. Though still subject to harassment and jailing today, the church has now become too big to suppress or contain in the future. May the chaos be with it.

Disclaimer: This chapter is included for sociological interest only and readers are advised to avoid any spiritual activity not supervised by ordained priests and sanctioned by the government. Then you will be sure to go to heaven - when you die.

It's 7am at a local church benefit in Goa

At the 1997 Reclaim The Streets party, held in London's Trafalgar Square.
1998 has seen scores of RTS parties staged around the country and across the world.

28. Positive Protest- get fluffy!

It is the growing perception of many on this planet that our society and civilization in the late twentieth century could be compared to a ship that is slowly sinking, or is in such rough waters that sinking is a distinct possibility. Some in our society are trying to repair the damage, building organizations and even new lifestyles that do not threaten the planet. The state reacts by passing laws to hamper activity of this sort and issues blanket assurances that all is well. If we were on an actual ship, the state would certainly have banned lifeboat construction long ago. Perversely, the state's behaviour can sometimes stimulate these activities, not to mention our overall feeling of disquiet.

Whether they are correct or not, those who feel a sense of responsibility for our civilization will react to this perceived danger by considering and experimenting with alternative lifestyles and prompting change in the status quo. They will also seek to make their voices heard over the blind assurances of the state that everything is being done for our own good and has been democratically rubber-stamped.

Were it not for those people who perceive problems before they become tragedies, society would indeed have a very rocky road to follow. Though bell-ringers of impending disaster are not always right, they should always be heard and considered. Why is it that every nuclear accident or release of toxins to the environment is accompanied by the familiar voice of the state assuring us that there has been no risk to public health or safety? As long as there is a seven year old inner-city child alive without asthma , we will be told by straight-faced government scientists that there is no "scientific proof " of a connection between increasing air pollution and rising asthma levels in children.

We vitally need the early warnings of those who are dismissed too often as scaremongers, cranks or some sort of an under-class of dissatisfied troublemakers. There are too many examples to mention of widely noted whistle blowers from Rachel Carson (*Silent Spring*) to Prof. Richard Lacey who warned of Mad Cow Disease.** They, and many others, were dismissed by authority and much of the public but later were tragically shown to be right. These people are not cranks - they question the status quo and prod us from our inclination to complacency when our lives are threatened. Is this not a better service to society than the banks of government-employed scientists sworn to the Official Secrets Act and working to who knows what agenda?

*This ground-breaking book, published in 1962, was the first to blow the whistle on the destruction of our natural habitat through excessive use of agro-chemicals - primarily DDT at the time.

**This respected scientist clearly pointed out the risks and dangers of Mad Cow Disease many years before the government that ridiculed him took any action to contain it.

As nation states throughout the world have become more oppressive in their ways we have seen a disturbing move to violence among those who seek to make their voice heard over attempts to silence dissent. Protest becomes frightening when demonstrators with twisted faces are throwing bottles and shouting obscenities at the other side. Such behaviour is alien to most of us, and often clouds our perception of the issue as we seek to distance ourselves from their actions. However, after the disillusioning failure of the CND* movement in the 60's, many lost hope in non-violent direct protest as a vehicle of change and either gave up, approached it from different angles or joined a left-wing group dedicated to becoming the next state by whatever means possible.

*The Campaign for Nuclear Disarmament, aiming to BAN THE BOMB, mobilized massive numbers and numerous highly respected figures and intellects of the fifties and sixties. Inspired by Gandhi's non-violence ethic, the protesters would sing rather than sling; their best known tactic was to go limp upon arrest and have to be dragged or carried away. The nuclear arms race continued until defused by the unexpected collapse of the Soviet bloc.

Around the world we see that when those without established power or influence are faced with gross injustice, they usually choose the techniques of those in power to try and gain attention for their cause. This has typically been through bombings, shootings, hijacking, organized militias, political assassination, hostage-taking, and the whole array of coercive techniques that have been the stock in trade of world leaders and would-be leaders throughout history.

Yet something very new and very powerful is developing, right now, here in Britain. A new culture has developed that is able to stage peaceful acts of dramatic civil disobedience that would have Thoreau, Tolstoy and Gandhi dancing in their graves. Compared to the just lie-down-and-go-limp tactics used by the unsuccessful CND movement of the early Sixties, today's aptly termed "eco-warriors" have advanced from the bow and arrow to the laser-guided smart bomb - if you will forgive the analogy. In the warrior tradition, they set strategies together, but act individually on the field of battle. It is now police practice to assemble a ratio of five police to one eco-warrior before commencing any action. One of the foundations of this power lies in the attitude defined by the word "fluffy," describing their non-coercive approach to dealing in face-to-face, fearless defiance of the full coercive powers of the state. It is not a passive strategy, and having fun is an important part of it. Regardless of where your thoughts lie on the roads issue, it is here that non-coercive direct action was fashioned into an effective working tool; one that the state may never develop a means to "deal with" to their satisfaction. So how did it come into existence?

One of the earliest sparks came at the spontaneous and inspired obstruction of a landscape-vandalizing road scheme across Twyford Down in 1993. A group of earth-loving people visiting the proposed road site, became appalled at the thoughtlessness with which the countryside was about to be destroyed, and were inspired to set up the country's first positively staged protest against a road. They came to call themselves the Dongas tribe, after the ancient paths and rights of way that once crossed that land. The final eviction, a black milestone in this country's history, involved four days of often brutal and violent removal by the police and security forces, with a spirited and dedicated resistance by the Dongas.

Twyford Down was followed by a passionate and prolonged battle to prevent a bypass destroying the beautiful Solsbury Hill outside of Bath. It is no longer there to enjoy. These early events became the first campaigns of the new eco-war that was to spread across the land following the historic "No-M11" campaign in East London. This year-long action culminated in the peaceful occupation and fortification of Claremont Road, the final street of residential houses waiting to be bulldozed for a 3-mile motorway link of dubious value- set to devour an entire neighbourhood of 300 houses. Most of the original residents had been

> Guardian - Apr 1996
>
> John Alderson, chief constable of Devon and Cornwall from 1973 to 1982, accuses Mr Howard of using the language of dictators like Hitler, Mussolini, and Franco: "Give me your liberties and I will protect you." ...
>
> "It is not in the nature of governments to grant liberty — they are all about power ... The present party political system is incapable of dealing with the challenges of society."
> He sees hope in the moral stand taken by anti-road and animal welfare groups, and particularly the women involved in them.

forced to sell and move out but a few held on defiantly and were soon joined by new neighbours, as the empty houses were occupied by squatters opposed to the building of this road. It became a lively community of people with two cheap vegetarian cafes, more exciting innovative art than you'll see at the Edinburgh Festival, and regular musical events and street parties. All this with a very low rent, though a high demand for courage, innovation, D.I.Y. culture and tolerance.

At the final siege on the 28th Nov.1994, after well over a year's occupation, some 200 eco-warriors, using strictly fluffy tactics, held the then remaining twelve houses against an army of 700 heavily equipped police, 300 bailiffs and 400 security guards for a full five days. This dramatic and lengthy final siege/eviction was accompanied by surprisingly few scenes of violence or ugly confrontation, one injury from a fall, and a handful of arrests on which charges were pressed. The final defender to be taken was Phil, not burrowing deep in a tunnel, but plucked from his sleep atop the splendid tower of painted fluorescent scaffolding rising 70ft above the short row of houses. For the first few days, the well-concealed Dolly's Tunnel supplied energy for the sound system and essential supplies to the surrounded protesters. It was named after Dolly, the sharp and lucid 92-year old dear who had refused to leave her lifelong home ("they'll have to carry me out"). She regarded her unconventional new neighbours as modern heroes, fighting today's Battle of Britain against the mindless destruction of our habitat and history by road-building schemes that are often ill thought out, frivolous, or downright unnecessary. Many others in the local neighbourhood shared her views and gave their full support and love to the new community in their midst.

The now footloose residents of Claremont Rd took their empowering and inspired fluffy techniques with them, taught others, and turned into a multi-headed Hydra having fun staging unpredictable, theatrical, humorous, big-time FUN productions all over the country. In between they were busy setting up new communities in road-threatened woodlands, buildings awaiting eventual demolition, on waste-land, common land, and in premises selected from the abundant stock of unused state-owned buildings (old courthouses, social security offices and the like). Sometimes long vacant private properties or land are squatted as well and here they always seek, and sometimes obtain, the owners permission to stay there on the understanding that they will completely vacate at the drop of a hat, and keep the building from deteriorating.*

*The ethics of this may sit uncomfortably with many readers, as it would with this writer were not cases of its abuse so rare. I also suggest that in those "primitive" cultures which recognized owning the right <u>to use land</u>, but not ownership of the land itself, there may have existed customs and conventions that saw someone lose rights to the exclusive use of land which had for a period of years neither been enjoyed by them nor their tenants - left vacant and unattended.

Reclaim the Streets (RTS) arose from this crucible and went on to earn a well-deserved reputation for pulling off some of the most audacious and unbelievable street parties, in between their other ongoing activities, and loosely related events such as the monthly action by cyclists - Critical Mass. The most stunning was "Street Party 96" that had its own flyer distributed all over the country many weeks in advance. What was the fluffy spirit of Claremont Road to achieve here, with no violence and but one arrest? Nothing less than a giant unauthorized (illegal) street party at an undisclosed major London road, attended by thousands of positive party-goers - all right under the eyes of the police authorities, and in spite of their very determined efforts to stop this party from taking place.

The day before the party only four people knew its location; by two the next afternoon there were seven thousand people either at, or on the way to the 800 metre long M41 motorway link in west London's Shepherd's Bush. All six lanes in both directions were smoothly occupied, in a precision action coordinating a truckload of sand "broken down" in the lay-by, the sound system truck likewise, a cavalry of a hundred or more cyclists, some quickly erected tripods with people

suspended therein, and thousands of party-goers simultaneously pouring in from nearby tube stations, having assembled earlier at Liverpool St. Station on the other side of London. Then the police did an efficient and good-natured job of redirecting traffic for the afternoon and evening (with a fraction of the disturbance caused by a single IRA scare). They never donned their riot outfits but quipped: "Thanks for coming, hope you had a good time" to me and many others as we left before midnight. There were caterers at the party, lots of wandering entertainers, children's play-area, carpets thrown down for sitting, a high proportion of the non-status quo attending and, oh yes, two giant Mardi Gras-style moving ballroom gown constructions. One of these settled next to the throbbing sound system for the evening and, as the police helicopter hovered overhead, a pneumatic drill worked away under cover of its skirts and the nearby repetitive beat. This, in order to plant a tree in the fast lane of the motorway - a strongly poetic statement and much better than the usual arsenal of nastiness. It can be difficult for the practitioners of coercion to deal with such non-aggressive and doggedly determined opponents with nothing to lose, something that none of their training covered.

Many camps and even an academy of tree-living branched out around the country, increasingly being joined and supported by the older and respectable population of Middle England. These new "recruits" shared a concern over the loss of the countryside and, in contact, realized that these most unusual looking people were kind, thoughtful, polite, responsible and well-spoken examples of the human race - something they often remember with nostalgia from their early years when whole communities like this still existed.

Perhaps the most significant offspring of Claremont Road to date was the historic Third Battle of Newbury - waged without violence against the controversial and poorly planned Newbury Bypass route. Between July 1995 and January 1996 some 36 separate camps were built in the path of the proposed route, complete with treehouses, lock-ons, aerial walkways, kitchens, communication facilities, and all the other artefacts of this new mobile community. Many from the local area became involved; both police and guards frequently expressed their support for the protesters position. It eventually took a hugely costly, usually laughable, and sometimes frightening operation by the authorities to exert their will and secure access to the site for contractors Costain. Private security guards, apparently paid directly from

Whitehall, had access to confidential police records, and conducted surveillance reminiscent of that practised behind the former Iron Curtain. Phone-taps, infiltration, and all the usual tools of the state were much in evidence.

Soon after the thousands of acres of ancient Newbury woodland, historic battlefields, and the 36 protest camps along the route had been taken and levelled, the Minister of Transport responsible admitted publicly that the road protesters had it right and that the Newbury bypass should never have been built along that route. From the safety of retirement, he acknowledged that the well overdue U-Turn in this country's roads policy had been brought about in just a few years by direct action road protest. Though most of the individual battle-stands of this campaign have eventually fallen before the weight of the coercers, it was at Newbury that the war appeared to have been won.

Shortly thereafter, at the nearby Fairmile Camp on the route of the proposed A30 extension, the whole issue leapt into the nation's consciousness when one of the many fluffy and determined members of this unique community became a national celebrity as all the sheriffs men were unable to get Swampy out of the tunnel he continued to dig for his record 167 hours stint, only emerging of his own accord when he thought that his point had been made. The public's appetite for a symbolic hero needed to be satisfied and it fell to the well-qualified Swampy to be the first gem to emerge from this rich mine at the very edge of our culture.

Other fluffy actions have included the giant canvas mock-motorway somehow draped over the then transport minister's house in the early morning - symbolically laying a motorway over his back yard and house. To protest at the police-state powers granted by the Criminal Justice Act, a "Mystery Excursion" brought several busloads to a picnic held in the garden of the Home Secretary's country house, then held a mock trial in which he was found guilty on various counts. In another anti-CJA action, five audacious men scaled the rooftop of the Houses of Parliament of the eve of Guy Fawkes night.. Profiled against Big Ben, they unfurled a large banner, smoked a large joint and called the press on their mobile phone - coming down only as the cold rainy night progressed. No charges were made following any of the above actions.

Fluffy does not see people of any type as an enemy just because they wear a particular uniform, are a different colour or practice a strange religion. Fluffy does not invite baton charges nor incur them in most instances. Fluffy behaviour is seen to work better than violence and that is why it has become established as the preferred "modus operandi" for Britain's new breed of action-oriented bell-ringers. Fluffy is also adopted as a powerful guiding principle in life and relationships. Even the police show it increasing respect as they realize that they are unlikely to ever confront brick throwing, punching or even verbal abuse much stronger than "Get a real job" or "What will your grandchildren think."

Today's eco-warriors display a constant level of inspiration and innovation, evolving techniques that can be sometimes be likened to those of the martial art of T'ai Chi Chuan in which a minimum of graceful movement takes the opponent's energy and turns it back with even greater force. It is combined with a powerful commitment to a DIY* culture which takes personal responsibility for tasks in hand, without any defined leadership or hierarchical control structure.

* Originally, DIY referred to Do It Yourself home building and decorating. It is now applied to an entire lifestyle outside of the mainstream cultural norm.

As Merrick says in his book *Battle for the Trees*: "There's something very amusing and satisfying about using government laws successfully against a government." Humour, including the ability to laugh at the totalitarian aspirations of the state, while sticking a soft spanner in their works from time to time, seems to work better than outrage and paranoia. It certainly maintains morale, raised spirits and higher energy in its practitioners. Most of the techniques and tactics that have developed from this fluffy philosophy serve to disable the adrenal glands and confuse the responses of those who are sent to attack them. The protesters universally seek to treat the police, bailiffs or security guards as human beings rather than the enemy.

Fluffy action is working. It is having an effect on the mainstream culture as millions of so-called "ordinary citizens" realize that valid points are being made by articulate and committed people, without using violence to gain attention. A major scaling down of superfluous road schemes has already taken place and their future development will never be quite so carefree again. General awareness has risen on the issues of air-pollution, animal welfare, nuclear power and our shrinking personal freedom. When the full costs of some of this century's follies are counted by future generations I do not wonder who will be looked upon as the villains and who as the heroes of the late twentieth century.

As this new type of protest has developed, the British state has passed - and continues to draft - seriously repressive new legislation designed to make criminal all the aspects of Britain's emerging new culture of which they disapprove. The Criminal Justice Bill 1994 was carefully designed to suppress techno music parties, the right to assembly, the right to protest, and anything else that got up the state's nose. Techno music was legally described as "wholly or predominantly characterized by the emission of a succession of repetitive beats." Look out Bach lovers, you might be next. In the recently rubber-stamped Police Bill, the police are given powers, for instance, to immediately close down any club at which they "suspect" that drug use or

Here comes
THE CRIMINAL JUSTICE BILL

'Wholly or predominantly characterised by the emission of a succession of repetitive beats.'

Kate Brown

trading is going on. They will also be allowed to bug or even burgle anyone who they suspect to be guilty of the "serious offence" defined as being one of "a large number of persons in pursuit of a common purpose." Perhaps Britain's new batch of rulers will roll back some of this tyranny.

Typically, the effect of the legislation passed to date has not exactly been what the government intended. It has served instead to weld together the hundreds of different groups at which it was targeted and thereby to spawn literally thousands more in their wake. At one point the British group LIBERTY was registering nine new groups to stop the bill's passage being formed per day. The "movement" or whatever you choose to call it, has never been stronger or more networked. Thank you Mr. Michael Howard, ex Home Secretary.

Indeed, Britain should be actively exporting this new fluffy technol-

ogy that peacefully and successfully promotes change and self-responsibility. It may well turn out to be one of the most successful mechanisms on the planet today for confronting the implacable face of the
state, regardless of financial status.

*Disclaimer: Readers are advised not to take part in any activities,
gatherings, parties or protests proscribed by the Criminal Justice
Act 1994, or any other official regulation. If you really want to be
happy in life then just stick to the rules, do what you're told, and
don't try thinking for yourself.*

29. A Working Example

I have made much of the ability of society to rise to the challenge of providing for its needs non-coercively when given a chance. I have also sought to convince overcome your fear of the void - to let go of your own inability as an individual to imagine the complex structures that would fill the holes left by the state's ineptitude and eventual decline.

It is not the remit of this book to conceive or predict the structures that will be necessary to replace the state's failing services, but let me take an example from the past which I have already mentioned once or twice. I refer to an industry that would be impossible to imagine if it did not already exist; which provides just the sort of service that we would expect our government to provide. It has done so and managed to usually make a profit at it, since it began some three hundred years ago. It is a different type of organisation from most and does not employ limited liability as a defence against mistakes or incompetence; and, just like the government, it doesn't sell you some easily identified product or service.

Have you guessed it yet or do you take the *insurance* business so much for granted that you never thought much about it? What insurance actually does is buy your risks, worries and fears from you. Since you view these things as being negative in value, you pay them instead of the other way around. So you can actually buy a product that provides for your family if you die, buys you a new car if the one you spent five years' savings on gets totalled, or supplies top-grade wigs and compensation for any customers going bald with your hair shampoo. You can get cover against it raining on your outdoor event or against a broken nose if you are a supermodel. Incredible service isn't it? And one you buy in the hope that you never have to use it.

This industry didn't develop as a result of any government initiative other than our own natural desire to create social and enterprise structures that help in the governing of our lives on all levels. The insurance industry started at a coffee-house in London called Lloyd's, which was frequented regularly by merchants and shipowners. At some point in the late 17th century one of them, or perhaps Edward Lloyd himself, had the idea that the individuals in the group could get rid of the ever-present risk of personal financial ruin if somehow the group shared the risk. Rather than ask everybody to put something in the pot to cover any eventualities, which might have caused some resistance, they jointly agreed to pay out whatever portion of a risk they shared, only if it came to pass. So that they would hopefully never need to dip into their pockets, a charge was made to each shipowner or merchant based on the value of what was insured and an estimate of the risk. It was a small cost of business since most ships and cargoes did come through.

I will avoid more detail on the wonderful mechanics that enable this industry to maintain enough money to cover the risks they promise to cover, without squandering it all on administration and overheads. I will not dwell on the exceptional cases we read of, when insurers have dishonoured the spirit of their contracts. Like you, I hope they go out of business, and avoid using any company suspected of operating that way. But the insurance industry, the worldwide industry that covers our risks in life, willingly pays out billions every year to enable the rebuilding of lives, homes, factories and farms that have been destroyed by the unpredictable. It is a governmental type of service that works, that evolves to cover new risks, and that manages to do so in a self-sustaining manner without the need to force our money from us. And when they pay a claim we are not made to feel like some supplicant receiving their blessing. The insurance industry is far from perfect - but it continues to survive and evolve by serving a purpose, as does everything else in the natural world. This industry is used as an example specifically because it does just the sort of thing that the state seeks to convince us only it can do.

Today, as we sit around in coffee houses, pubs, think-tanks or boardrooms, discussing the problems facing society, we are most often channelled into a fruitless, head-banging wander down a one-way street. When the discussion turns to subjects like crime, education, health, homelessness or pollution, we end up thinking within the framework of the state. The problem is addressed in terms of the proposed legislation, restrictions and subsidies that are put on the table by either the In Party or the Out party. We sort again and again through the "terminal toolbag" looking for a magic way to make these devices work. This is because we accept the monopoly the state exerts in these areas and somehow expect it to lead us forward rather than hold us back. We must now embrace the alternative option, which is to begin building more structures that are as simple and self-perpetuating as the insurance industry. We do not need to predict or determine exactly the highly developed form they will have assumed with twenty years evolution from the original idea. We can be sure though that as we recognise new needs the solutions will be sought.

I also freely admit that the incredible technological tools now available and the personal powers which they give us, make the self-management of our complex society a much more real and attainable concept today than it may have been a century ago. It is understandable that the existing states of the world fear, and seek to suppress, developments such as the Internet, since the technological freedom to communicate and create a community that is free of bureaucratic control poses a genuine threat to their continued grip upon our world society.

"Liberty means responsibility.
That is why most men dread it."

George Bernard Shaw (1856 - 1950)

30.   Some Other Directions

As I said in the first chapter, this book does not propose to offer answers to all the challenges that face us. But as we have seen in the insurance industry, society can develop a mechanism to provide all of society with the sort of service that we might imagine requires a coercive state to manage. This chapter puts forward some "imaginings" of overall governing structures, or principles no more complex or arcane than those of the insurance industry; structures that might develop in a climate where needs arise in society, needs which are no longer the preserve of the state to manage. It should even be possible to build some of them alongside the state's faltering structures

The most universal and essential product group of all is the food that we eat, usually more than once every day of our lives, regardless of where we live. Of course we need standards for our foods so we can guard against botulism in our canned food and be sure that the ingredients listed on a food packet are complete and accurate. We want to know that when a product is sold as organically grown, it fits some definition of organic that satisfies us. And we want to be sure that our food is not contaminated with heavy metals, toxic bacteria, rat droppings or other noxious contaminants.

Though the state would have us believe that it looks after all the above and more, today's increasingly conscious consumers are becoming more aware of the flimsiness of the state's protection, a state whose own involvement in the food chain has often led to dangers far more endemic and frightening than rat shit or even a touch of heavy metal. Typically the state will try to deny or cover up such dangers, assuring us that there has been no risk to human health. Occasionally they will actually suggest that consumers, if they want to be absolutely sure, should maybe buy a few less carrots or apples and be sure to peel them, or something like that. Then, one suspects, they take steps to ensure that such information does not unexpectedly leak out again in the future.

Where consumers are unconcerned about their food quality, no amount of regulations will make much difference in the quality of their diet. However, in many countries today, as more and more consumers recognise the connection between their health and their food chain, there certainly exists a market for a company - perhaps an extension of an existing consumer association - whose remit is to provide genuine product certification to food producers, incorporating regular testing of their product. This can be done with bonded personnel able to review a company's working recipes, relative to ingredient listing. It is in the interests of the food industry to have a standard of integrity that is trusted by the public. If such a standard is developed and maintained by a private organisation, its own existence will be threatened if it devalues its integrity by colluding with a food company to condone false or misleading data. In today's society there is always the chance of such activity leaking to a newspaper or TV investigator. If something is of value then it gets paid for, in this instance the most likely funding would be from a modest charge pro rata to volume sales of an individual company. There can be alternative validation schemes available so, for instance, separate companies may deal with organic or cruelty-free claims from those validating ingredient and nutritional contents.

But the intention here is not to map out each specific of how such a company might run or how it might deal with all the ifs and buts that any critic of such a concept could easily raise. Let's also not pretend we're so stupid that, if we are interested, we'll be confused by some jungle of different symbols. Such an industry is by its nature likely to standardise, though it may (or may not) begin with a confusing array of symbols. In the author's experience, however, when a consumer seeks to be assured that a product is free of animal products, or wheat gluten, or some or all chemical additives, or is produced without cruelty or is Kosher, then that consumer is willing to look for the symbol. Something similar has developed in the travel industry, without government intervention, with an international coding that lets you know everything about an hotel from the number of beds, to disabled access, to swimming pool or golf course, and catering facilities. At an even simpler level the vetting company can guarantee, like a company auditor, that everything the manufacturer says on the label is wholly true, accurate and not misleading.

Naturally, in the absence of state control, such a scheme would not be a mandatory requirement for all food manufacturers. Many retailers would choose to demand it of their large suppliers whilst performing in-house vetting of the small manufacturers, who keep supermarket shelves interesting and changing (and are easier to inspect at one small unit). Some brands' credentials might be so beyond reproach as to not need any outside standard, though such a manufacturer is probably likely to support it most. What we achieve with this service is another important weave added to the web of our food supply system, providing rapid feedback from the public to the food suppliers about the changing needs and perceptions of that society. This is not something that the state's management can ever provide.

In the same way, we are perfectly capable as a society to develop standards and means to ensure that our cigarette lighters do not explode in our face, that our cars run at the promised m.p.g., that dye-fast clothes do not run nor babies' mattresses explode into flames. While there should be no restrictions on appointing whomever we like (including ourselves) to act in "professional" areas for us, we are able to ensure through various accreditations or associations that our lawyer, doctor, publisher or trade mark agent has met certain standards of responsibility and expertise that we desire. Of course, we are usually more likely to be swayed by a good reputation and personal recommendation. Though obstructed by jealous state control of standards,* we should soon see an even greater development of independent product certification companies providing customer guarantees with responsibility. So you won't have to visit the farm to make sure your carrots are organic or check the stated "pH factor" on the soap you use.

* The American Heart Association recently initiated a scheme to certify and label saturated fat content in consumer food products. The Food and Drug Administration promptly slapped them down, as although no such information appeared on packs in any standard format, this was the responsibility of the FDA and not something to be handled otherwise.

No standards are of much use without a form of written codes, and regulations that govern the action to be taken in the case of their wilful or accidental transgression. Let's just look at civil law for now, which often does not involve coercion but requires some form of redress for damage, injury, poor service or break of guarantee. Though it might be more complex, it is quite possible for a system to evolve whereby companies and individuals making business exchanges, are voluntarily part of a large Assurance House that operates codes of conducts, regulation and law applying to their interactions; companies abide by this or lose their reputation and their ability to work within the business community. Integrity, guarantees, and liabilities can be financially backed by the "Assurance House," who may even require security from some customers. Support of this organization would be a basic cost of doing business for many, though street vendors, church fete sales, start up concerns and others may choose not to be bonded or to undertake some simpler and less reassuring scheme. The buyer must always exercise some intelligence and discrimination, as goes the old adage "let the buyer beware."

The already vast mechanism of practical civil law, which includes the use of arbitrators, does not need the additional weight of the state to support and maintain. Most companies, large and small, work with an extensive base of existing contracts and codes that are accepted and expected. Some companies and people work on a simple handshake, knowing their honour is enough assurance. Others can draft devious contracts that "legally" cheat the other side out of what was expected, or will openly break the agreement and challenge the aggrieved party to try and sue for justice through the courts at great expense. I do not intend to elaborate on how contracts could be guaranteed and the existing structure improved, other than that it will take the co-operation of banks and business as well as some new types of assurance and bonding companies. I believe the need for this to be so great that a solution will be created within business in order to ensure the ongoing survival and effectiveness of trade. Much of the structure that is required already exists.

Without the state, I hear you cry, who will tell us which side of the road to drive upon. Come on! With today's technology, and a privately owned or operated roads system we could figure out not only which side to drive on, but be charged according to just how much road is being used, based on some vehicle-type and mileage scale. We can also look forward to real attempts to reduce the scale of car pollution, since a private road company must eventually meet the costs of paying for environmental pollution caused by its operation, and face the risk of being sued for asthma cases in young children. According to one study, some 75% of road pollution is caused by just 20% of the vehicles on the road - not so hard to make a big difference. Imagine how much more efficient will be the use of motor vehicles when road usage is charged according to the demands made upon the road, rather than according to a ridiculous flat road tax system that charges the same to a customer driving 50,000 miles per year as to one driving 1,000. A private road company is also far less likely to treat its customers as the enemy to be trapped, fined and clamped for profit. Neither is a private company so likely to build unwanted new roads, when existing ones can be improved and maintained. Useless roads cost money to build, especially without the handy tool of compulsory purchase (read coercive for compulsory). Consider too, under private ownership, how long ago we would have developed truly intelligent traffic lights, rather than ever more complex intersections; lights that never had drivers stopping, idling and re-accelerating (causing needless pollution and road wear) when there was absolutely no reason to do so. Instead, we find needless traffic lights now destroying the smooth function of that great British invention - the roundabout.

And at last, we might use our wonderful technology to develop a machine that tests automobile drivers for whether or not they are competent to drive, rather than for a linear level of alcohol or any other substance. Someone on antibiotics and a glass of wine can be lethal - as can anyone dulled to near sleeplessness by Valium or other prescribed drugs. Really, there are enough pharmaceuticals to be tested for to justify posting a chemist and laboratory in every patrol van. The only sensible way to keep dangerous drivers off the road is to test whether they are dangerous or not with a cheap and universally accurate device that measures response, reaction, and motor coordination.

Another area of great concern is the control and reduction of crime without increased policing and incarceration. To this end I will hint at the principles that might help us develop solutions; whether the eventual mechanisms fit any predetermined format or whether such formats can be described now is not relevant. What is relevant is the knowledge that a complex system, such as society, has the tendency to develop means to govern and stabilize itself without falling into disorder and entropy.

And though it may not seem obvious, it is very much in the interests of the giant worldwide insurance industry to combat crime. The bulk of the industry supplies cover against risks of death, disaster, misfortunes, and unexpected events that involve no malevolent acts of mankind. As well as natural events, cover is also supplied against the risk of being robbed or injured in the course of a crime. Though some might argue that rising crime is good for the insurers because they get more policies from frightened people, we see this is starkly not the case in high crime American inner-city areas where crime is so bad they will not insure. There is no joy at the insurance office when a client is robbed or murdered, or when crime figures rise - any more than there is glee at increased hurricanes, fires, bus crashes or floods. When these events occur, so does a cost and a deduction from profits - when they occur too often then the insurer ultimately risks losing their shirt, since limited liability does not apply. Much of the industry growth today comes from new insurance such as that which comes with everything purchased on some credit cards, or bad weather insurance for outdoor events, or other areas where there may not be any exploitation of your fear - just a means to offset a perfectly straightforward risk.

Since the main cost to insurance companies is payouts to customers who make claims, their greatest interest is in reducing the number of claims. The point being made is: when the insurance companies start to build tools with which to prevent crime and pursue criminals they will not be victims of the "terminal toolbag" syndrome. They have nothing to gain from increasing crime and everything to gain from its reduction. They have nothing to gain from putting people in jail for crimes that have no victims, nor in putting the wrong people in jail just to secure a conviction. Indeed they have everything to gain from reducing the need for expensive jails as the main plank of their strategy to deter criminals from crime.

> ## Polluters warned of equity pullout
>
> **Paul Brown in Kyoto**
>
> EUROPEAN and Asian insurance companies, which are among the world's biggest stock owners, warned environment-damaging companies yesterday that they will unload their shares if they do not mend their ways.
>
> The insurance industry, which controls £10,000 billion in equities, a third of the value of global stockmarkets, held a press briefing as a "counter-weight" to the fossil-fuel lobby, which publicly admits that it wants to wreck the climate talks in Kyoto.
>
> Guardian - Dec 1997

The insurance companies may need other allies from the business world and it is not hard to recognize that, with the assistance of the banking world, it would be very difficult for criminals, once detected, to enjoy the proceeds of their crimes. The world of business must certainly recognize that society's desire for a climate of reducing crime and immorality is an opportunity for profit to themselves, greater in the long term than that afforded by its proliferation. I am not proposing here just how this would work.* I am just pointing out that, should the opportunity arise, there are possibilities for the non-coercive part of our society to take an interest in (and actions that will lead towards) the ultimate objective of steadily reducing crime, rather than simply building an industry that feeds upon the growing problem.

*A concept developed at length by Professor Galambos - see Credits.

Taking a great leap of imagination, let us assume that we have some-how finally arrived at the idyllic situation where there are no states in the world to threaten our (now dissolving) borders, coercively dictate how we behave, all the time emptying our pockets of as much as they can. So how, in this bliss, do we ensure that another Hitler or Pol Pot does not secretly amass an army, build his own weapons, and overrun the nearest defenceless neighbour to hand? Surely someone needs to keep a large military force to guard against this threat and, moreover, how do we protect ourselves from some miscreant gaining control of this protective military machine unless we all have our own standing armies. Sounds a bit pessimistic? Consider extending the concept out-lined for dealing with crime, so that it includes the cooperation of the telecommunication companies and the power companies; then it be-comes virtually impossible for anyone to amass such a force and do anything seriously destructive with it against a world full of free people with industries that are independent, interdependent and connected naturally by a working network of their own feedback.

These are but leaps of imagination and I do not pretend to anticipate the means which humanity and the chaos of free selection will use to create the order and stability we seek, and rightly expect to govern vital aspects of our society. They do also rely upon an assumption by busi-ness of a level of morality to which most leaders of industry would pro-fess, but to which few adhere. Whilst this might sound idealistic, it is more realistic than hoping that this level of morality will ever develop in the thought or actions of the world's political leaders. The corporate world of today, however entwined with the state on some levels, is still largely dependent upon the free wishes of the billions of people in this world and tends usually to produce the products that we demand. We have a choice.

*"The mystery of government
is not how Washington works
but how to make it stop."*

*P.J. O'Rourke
Parliament of Whores*

31. Emptying the Corridors of Power

The old adage goes: "Don't vote, it only encourages them." True, but many nation states now make voting a mandatory requirement, and those that do not will still assume the mantle of "the majority" when less than a quarter of the population have supposedly given them a mandate. I say supposedly, because the balance is nearly always tipped by people voting <u>against</u> someone else rather than <u>for</u> anyone. Many of today's non-voters do so (or don't do so) out of disgust with the whole charade, but the system just counts them as apathetic, ignoring their non-vote. The system meanwhile just trundles on as if everything was going according to plan, and a working party is set up to find ways of getting more people to appreciate the value of their vote.

Many of England's new breed of fluffy activists have found ways to enmesh and embroil the state in its own convoluted laws and regulations, which it must regularly break in order to deal with the protesters. Notice how often the charges are dropped shortly after arrests are made. Perhaps there is a way to use the sacred "right" to vote itself as the tool with which we disempower the state. Perhaps there is a way to retract the people's mandate altogether. What would happen if there were a way to vote <u>against</u> the politicians themselves, rather than just picking one from the selection?

Well, I did have an idea on this some years ago, the memory of which was revived in the writing of this book. It arose as a result of a commitment I made to my eccentric friend Rainbow George one night. Somehow he got me, a dedicated non-politico, to agree to launch a political party of some sort at his next Rainbow Alliance press conference. There was a local by-election involved, and George kept phoning to remind me of my promise.

As the event drew near, I put my mind to the problem one evening and drafted the skeleton of a platform for which it would seem worth casting a vote. Then, it was named the No-Candidate Party, and I was "Gregory Sams - not standing for Parliament." I printed up a press release and cards with "Political De-activist" printed under my name. It got a mention in a few newspapers and a radio interview but never went any further at the time.

It could be renamed as the Bare Seat Party or the NOTA Party (None

Of The Above). The party headquarters would have a binding standard form of agreement signed with any prospective candidate. This single-sheet agreement goes something along the lines of: "I undertake, if elected, never to attend a session of parliament nor vote on any issue in any way, nor in any way perform any of the duties of office. I undertake never to encash any payments forthcoming as wages, salary or remuneration from the state, nor claim any travel rights, expenses or jobs for relatives, friends or strangers."

Each vote for the BARE SEAT PARTY would be a vote for one less politician, sending shudders down the corridors of power, followed by a disturbing tremor should a single seat in Parliament be emptied in this way. It is a vote against all of the parties currently vying for control. It also stops anyone from assuming that you don't vote because you are just too lazy or apathetic to take part in the exciting process of choosing a bunch of new faces to create yet more legislation and break unkeepable promises for the next however-many years.

This new party is not presented as some sort of ultimate technique for unravelling the state but as a simple and effective part of getting the process rolling - a catalyst and a spur to other more important and relevant action that is not even determinable at this time. It could well prompt the business and general community to initiate more construction of working alternatives to the 20% of the state's work that is essential to our society. One less politician is no big deal in itself, but if brought about by the vote and not a bullet or a bomb then it would be something genuinely new in the political world, and a sign to its practitioners that they had better start looking for real jobs in the medium term future.

> "What politics is really about is a lot of mirrors and blue smoke. People have power when other people think they have power. If they don't think that, then you're an empty vessel."
>
> Whych Fowler, American politician quoted 1978

The suggestion presented here makes your vote send a powerful signal to the state and guarantees that you will never be mis-represented by your candidate. A vote for the Bare Seat Party sends the strongest possible message to the state that we are fed up with their antics and that their power is receding.

No Bare Seat Party exists at the time of writing and this author is neither familiar with, nor competent at, such organization building. The concept is very simple and could in theory be applied anywhere in the world. I have no idea of how funding for deposits and whatever else would be obtained, and hope that anyone undertaking such an important venture would find a means to profit from its success.

Disclaimer: For their own health and happiness, as well as ours, all readers are advised never to get mixed up in politics, and never to run for public office.

THE NO CANDIDATE PARTY

Gregory Sams

NOT STANDING FOR PARLIAMENT

IT SAYS MORE
THAN NOT VOTING
VOTE FOR NONE OF THEM!

Our franchise is the people who now realize that the left and the right are both wings of the same bird - that however far to the left or right you go, or whether you opt for the middle - *the bird does not fly!*

We have no hairbrained platform - no policy. Vote for us if you actively **do not want** to be represented by the cranks and lunatics who purport to run the country. All we aspire to is our deposit back. We will not drain, control, or manipulate the economy.

A VOTE FOR ONE LESS BUREAUCRAT

The No Candidate Party

supporting
the Rainbow Alliance

Gregory Sams
Tel: 01
Tlx 94016334

1988

"The time is always right to do what is right."

Martin Luther King, Jr. (1929 - 1968)

32. And Where From Here?

I do not mean to suggest that all our problems are caused by the state and its institutions but I would suggest that most of them are; I also maintain that if we were neither financing these institutions nor suffering their inevitable negative side-effects, we as a world society would eventually create the structures we need in order to live safe, happy, healthy and unthreatened lives.

We do need structures as complex as the insurance industry or the airline industry and they must in many cases be built from scratch. We already see society seeking to escape the state's failings in areas such as healthcare, in which an entire alternative industry, offering therapies ranging from Bach Flower Remedies to Chinese Herbalism, has been built from nothing in 20 years. It is highly noteworthy that these new medical industries have thrived in a free market - despite the fact that their main competition, the NHS, is provided as a "free service". Private security firms have also prospered as the state becomes less able to protect us from robbery and attack. These industries are being funded by customers who must continue, in most cases, to pay for the state's diminishing service. Imagine how much more we could achieve if we only had to pay once, and only for the service we want.

It will also take an attitude change among business leaders. We see this taking place already as increasing numbers of companies pay attention to environmental and health concerns, taking positive action long before being required to do so by government legislation. They have friends and children too, and a public image that is often built on something real and meaningful. It is unfortunate but understandable that business sometimes apes the state in its effort to determinedly retain a coercive grip on its market, in a climate where those who run the state are perceived as leaders. When they also recognise that such an approach is unprofitable they will at least seek other models. Many business leaders today are as disenchanted with the state as are the road-protesters living in a bender of tree-house. From a long-term viewpoint the evidence indicates that the state's coercive techniques have a built-in unprofitability factor, and that we are the losers.

I also optimistically put some trust in human nature - this is because I have usually found the raw material to be worthy of that trust. I believe that when responsibility for morality is taken from the immoral state and returned to society, our society will be able to construct a means to recover its lost integrity, and engineer a return to safe environments with less police and jails, not more. These police will perhaps come to be funded by the insurance industry who can only profit by reduced levels of crime and danger. Criminals who steal things don't get much use out of their plunder without the support of the banks. Banks, too, need to address their responsibilities to society and to recognise the **long-term profitability of morality** in a climate where they are permitted to take a long term view.

There has been much serious and worthwhile study of mechanisms in a genuine free market that could deal with some of the seemingly intractable problems we would confront without a state. An example is how to deal effectively with coercive crimes in a non-coercive manner. This and many other issues have been addressed, though in many cases the self-supporting structure that needs to be built may not fit into the legislative definition of what is acceptable to the tax authorities, who force all enterprise into one of a few narrow and carefully defined formats.

We can do it. We have the tools and the intellect to advance our civilisation. It is unlikely that we can do it however while still carrying the monkey of the state on our backs, diverting the resources that we have generated into ever more distorting and damaging schemes, hopeless programmes and deadly confrontations with other monkeys.

As I said in the beginning, this book isn't proposing a new way to run the world because there is no way to "run" such a complex system. In his satirical novel "**1984**", George Orwell warned us of the possible future in an "ideal" Soviet world. Perhaps unwittingly, he came close to depicting the uniform society and permissible "headset" to which many statesmen today would seem to aspire - albeit with fuller refrigerators and colour TV. It is now apparent, however, that it is beyond anybody's powers to accomplish such control, be they saint or Stalin, and that what we, humanity, are suffering today is the result of the fumbling and dangerous attempts of the state to achieve its dream version of George Orwell's nightmare.

That which we most reliably enjoy today is the fruit of our own complex and chaotic society, not the creation of any parliament, king or emperor. We can live happily within our complex system and we can find ways to govern and manage some of the more universal elements of it.

I can make but a few suggestions on how we regain our freedom from the state and on how we correct or unravel the iniquities of history. This is a job for the complex system to address. It is certainly not a job for any politician who asks for your vote on the promise of reducing the state; but if we are to govern or influence this system successfully, we must recognise that we cannot do so using coercion as our basic tool. If we seek to attack the state and are somehow successful, we then become the next state. Do not attack the state. Just live without it as the focus and build to survive its decay.

Credits

In my own near half century on this planet I have always sought the new and the unusual, often being exposed to and embracing ideas years, even decades before they began to assume a popular impact on the culture. This has not stopped me, ever, from appreciating the old and traditional - though not for the sake of its being old or traditional. I have, during this time, studied how new ideas emerge and penetrate the culture, often helping with the process.

Though life itself is the ultimate teacher, the main signposts have been indicated to me by Charles Fort, Georges Ohsawa, Professor Galambos and the findings of the early workers in chaos theory such as Benoit Mandelbrot and Edward Lorenz. These great men's ideas have been assimilated with those of my forward-thinking parents and countless other teachers, pioneers and friends, then tested against my observations of life and our society on the planet.

Charles Fort made me realise that many events in the world are unexplained by any known science or thought system, and that serendipity and coincidence are not nearly as random as I would have thought. He was my first exposure to the notion of the "Butterfly Effect," though I hardly absorbed it from his obtuse example which ran something like "not a bottle of ketchup can fall from a tenement window in New York that will not affect the price of rice in China."

Georges Ohsawa taught me about self-responsibility and the importance of food in our lives. He taught me that food was anything consumed through the mouth, eyes, ears or other senses. My focus for many years was the food we put in our mouths, greatly enhanced by the natural food upbringing my parents, Kenneth and Margaret, gave me. This led to me bringing the first brown rice into the country in 1967 and eventually launching the original "all natural-all vegetable" VegeBurger® in 1982, with many other "firsts" in between. My understanding of self-responsibility at an early age was also immensely helpful in dealing with life from a wheelchair, after breaking my back in 1966 at the age of 18.

Professor Galambos' lessons made me realise that we will not, as a society, be able to eat our way out of the problems that face us. He alerted me to the basic failings of coercion as a tool of state and taught me about the profitability of morality and the morality of profitability. His definition of PROFIT is "any increase in happiness obtained through moral action." I discovered that right wing and left wing are but different tilts of the same bird. Galambos in particular, figured out coercion-free mechanisms that could successfully be run by us as a society, in order to manage the areas that the state has monopolised for many years. I found out about the Wright Brothers and how insurance works. He also made me realise how much I had to gain by fully appreciating the value to me of the ideas of men who explored new thought, men such as Archimedes, Bruno, Galileo, Isaac Newton, Thomas Paine and Nicola Tesla. Though almost unheard of today, Andrew J. Galambos belongs in this select group.

Discovering chaos theory in 1990 brought together all the currents of my life to date - and introduced me to one of the greatest principles of this universe. It made immediate sense of all life's wonderful synergy when I recognised that it was the nature of the universe to create harmony and beauty. I rapidly perceived the significance of the discoveries of chaos theory to our society and saw how we thwart the constructive energies of chaos (as in the Greek XAOS) by seeking to forcibly govern it. I wanted to make sure that these discoveries would not remain in the province of the hard sciences and would be recognised as operating in our society as well as the rest of the universe. I opened Strange Attractions, the world's first shop dedicated to chaos theory, passing it to other hands (Thornton Streeter) after two years. Since then I have pursued the path of a successful fractographer and artist responsible for hundreds of thousands of fractally decorated posters and other products, and for literally tens of millions of imprints in magazines and publications around the world.

It is my hope that an understanding of this new science called chaos theory will by now have reached sufficiently into the popular culture for this book to fall on receptive ears. We have lost much progress following in the failed footsteps of the past. If we are to survive and prosper into the future it will only be when we take responsibility for that future ourselves.

Big Butterflies

A few names stand out of the seamless passage of chaos; people who triggered important changes in my life - sometimes through simple contributions.

Special thanks to the late Dr. Nakadadi who set my mother and father on the wholefood path in the late 1940's, and to them for keeping to it. Also to my brother Craig who, in 1966, brought back news of Georges Ohsawa whose books on Macrobiotics had been burnt by the FDA - because he suggested that the "all-American" red meat & white starch diet was a tad dangerous.

For the introduction to A.J. Galambos' unique courses I must thank Kim Bockus, Evan R. Soulé and John Fountain who between them provided the stimulus and material.

During the VegeBurger days some great leaps forward were made through a lunch with Annette Middleton, a pint or two with Lindsay Vincent, and much time in the company of the always amazing Mister Switzer.

My immersion into chaos theory was prompted by artist Howie Cooke, and developed through my interactions with Peter Cox, Ernie, Filiz, Grant, and Jesse Jones who wrote the excellent fractal software called Mandella (also Mandelbrowser).

Thanks too in the inspirations department to Susannah, Martin, Phoenix, George, Des and their tribes; to Jeff, Hoppy, Sue Hall, Raja Ram and Bonnie for their part in many personal transformations; to my ex-wife Sandy for many things (including this book's title); to Sterling for his thorough rough draft review; to James for his relentless proof-reading, to SchNEWS for the disclaimer style, and to all of the friends and associates who have supported and encouraged my activities.

SOME BOOKS

A few books which have influenced or bear upon ideas raised in this book.

Briggs, John and Peat, David F., *Turbulent Mirror.* (Harper & Rowe, NY 1990)

Bryson, Bill, *Made in America.* (Secker & Warburg Ltd. London 1994)

Capra, Fritjof, *The Web of life.* (HarperCollins, London 1996)

Carson, Rachel, *Silent Spring.* (Hamish Hamilton, London 1963)

Cheney, Margaret, *Tesla - Man Out Of Time.* (Prentice-Hall Int. Inc. London 1981)

Davies, Paul, *God and the New Physics.* (Penguin Books Ltd, London 1983)

Drexler, Eric, *Engines of Creation.* (Anchor, U.S.A. 1987)

Duncan, Alan & Hobson, Dominic, *Saturn's Children.* (Sinclair-Stevenson 1995)

Ehrereich, Barbara, *Blood Rites.* (Virago Press, London 1997)

Fishall, R.T. *Bureaucrats- how to annoy them.* Arrow Books Ltd, London 1981)

Garcia, Linda, *The Fractal Explorer.* (Dynamic Press, Santa Cruz, Berkeley 1991)

Gleick. James.*Chaos.* (William Heinemann Ltd, London 1988)

Goldsmith, James, *The Trap* (Macmillan Ltd, London 1994)

Hauschka, Rudolf, *Nutrition (Rudolf Steiner Press,* London 1967)

Hofstadter, Douglas R. *Godel, Escher, Bach:* (Harvester, Great Britain 1979)

Huxley, Aldous, *The Doors of Perception and Heaven and Hell.* (Reissue Edition HarperCollins, London 1990)

Leary, Timothy, *Chaos and Cyberculture.* (Ronin Publishing, CA. 1994)

Mc Kenna, Terence, *Food of the Gods.* (Rider, Random Century, London 1992)

Merrick, *Battle for the Trees.* (Godhaven ink, po box hp94, Leeds LS6 1YJ)

Murray, William,J, *Anarchic Harmony.* (Loompanics, Port Townsend,WA .U.S.A.)

Ohsawa, George, *Zen Macrobiotics.* (Ohsawa Foundation Inc. Los Angeles, 1965)

Orwell, George, *Nineteen eighty-four.* (Penguin Books Ltd. London 1949)

Paine, Thomas, *Common Sense and The Crisis.* (Anchor Press, New York 1973)

Pauwels, Louis & Bergier, Jacques, *The Morning of the Magicians.* (Anthony Gibbs and Phillips Ltd, London 1963)

Prigogine, Ilya & Stengers, Isabelle, *Order Out of Chaos.* (Flamingo, Fontana Paperbacks London 1985)

Rand, Ayn, *Atlas Shrugged* and *The Fountain Head.* (Cassell & Co Ltd, GB 1947)

Schwenk, Theodor, *Sensitive Chaos.* (Rudolf Steiner Press, London 1965)

Stewart, Ian, *Does God play Dice?* (Penguin Books Ltd, 1990)

Tsu, Lao, *Tao Te Ching. (*Random House Inc. New York 1972)

Tzu, Sun, *The Art of War.* (Shambhala, Boston & London 1991)

Velikovsky, I., *Worlds in Collision,* (Abacus, 1977)

Watson, Lyall, *Supernature.* (Coronet, Hodder & Stoughton Ltd, London 1973)

Watts, Alan, *The Book - On the Taboo Against Knowing Who You Are.* (Random House Inc New York 1966)

Wong, Eva, *The Shambhala Guide to Taoism.* (Shambhala, Boston & London 1997)

OTHER Information:

SchNEWS (weekly newspaper): website: http:/www.cbuzz.co.uk/schNEWS/
Fortean Times: PO Box 2409, London NW5 4ND, England
A.J.Galambos teaching: Contact F.E.I. PO Box 181247, Coronado, CA 91278-1247
WEBSITE of Author's Fractal & Graphics at **http://www.tarcl.com/greg**
WEBSITE for chaOs worKs, and this book **http://www.xaos.demon.co.uk.**

The Golden Rule

Christianity:
All things whatsoever ye would that men should so to you,
do ye even so to them: for this is the Law and the Prophets.
Matthew, 7.12

Islam:
No one of you is a believer until he desires for his brother
that which he desires for himself.
Sunnah

Judaism:
What is hateful to you, do not to your fellow men. That is
the entire Law; all the rest is commentary.
Talmud, Shabbet, 31a

Brahmanism:
This is the sum of duty: Do naught unto others which would
cause you pain if done to you.
Mahabarata, 51 1517

Buddhism:
Hurt not others in ways that you yourself would find hurtful.
Udan-Varga, 5,18

Confucianism:
Surely it is the maxim of loving-kindness: Do not unto others
that you would not have them do unto you.
Analects, 15.23

Taoism:
Regard your neighbour's gain as your own gain, and your
neighbour's loss as your own loss.
T'ai Shang Kan Ying Pien

Zoroastrianism:
That nature alone is good which refrains from doing unto
another whatsoever is not good for itself.
Dadistan-i-dinik, 94,5

re-originated from a T-shirt of unknown origin, seen by the author in Goa

BOOKSHOP SUPPLY

CENTRAL BOOKS - 91 Wallis Road, London E9 5LN
Tel: (44) 0181 986 4854
Fax (44) 0181 533 5821

OTHER SHOPS SUPPLY

KNOCKABOUT - 10 Acklam Road, London W10 5QZ
Tel: (44) 0181 969 2945
fax: (44) 0181 968 7614

MAIL ORDER

Uncommon Sense		ONE .... pack of copy .... FIVE
UK	2nd class	£ 8.00 .... £25.00
Europe		£ 8.50 .... £27.00
Worldwide	surface airmail	£ 8.50 .... £27.00 £10.00 .... not available

Send cheque, postal order, money order, Giro, or Eurocheque in Pounds Sterling. Sorry, but NO CREDIT CARDS.

PAYABLE to Chaos Works and mail to:
2 Trevelyan Gardens • London NW10 3JY • England
(be sure that YOUR ADDRESS is written CLEARLY in CAPITALS)

Cover and book design
by the author
with a little help
from his friends
using PageMaker on
an Apple Macintosh.
Photos and fractals by the author
with back cover photo by Antonia.